THE ULTIMATE

Scrap Quilt

JOYCE MORI

**krause
publications**

700 E. State Street • Iola, WI 54990-0001

krause publications

700 East State Street • Iola, WI 54990-0001
Telephone 715-445-2214

Please call or write for our free catalog of publications. Our toll-free number to place an order or obtain a free catalog is 800-258-0929 or please use our regular business telephone 715-445-2214 for editorial comment and further information.

Designed by Jan Wojtech
Photography by Edward A. Petrosky, West Virginia University Publications Service
Illustrations by Eric Merrill
Manufactured in the United States of America

Library of Congress Cataloging-in-Publication Data

Mori, Joyce
 The ultimate scrap quilt: create new "constructed" fabric from scraps—an easy and exciting new approach to creating quilts, blocks, and wearable art.

 Includes index.
 ISBN 0-8019-8925-6
 1. Quilting   2. Sewing   3. Title

 97-073029
 CIP

Acknowledgments

My deep appreciation to my husband John, who puts up with scraps and threads all over the house and quilts in progress on every flat space. I thank him for his advice on color ideas when I get stumped.

A thank you to Susan Keller who contributed many good ideas to the manuscript. She always has a positive and pleasant attitude. Special thanks to my editor Barbara Case who made the book clear and concise. I appreciate all her hard work.

Several of the quilt ideas were contributed by my friend Pat Hill, who lives in West Hills, California. Pat and I have never met but we became pen pals because of a mutual interest in quilts with Native American designs. Pat wrote this poem for her fellow quilters and she has allowed me to share it. I hope it comes true for all of you.

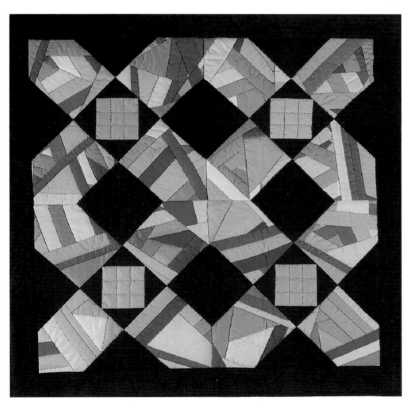

My Wish for Fellow Quilters

by Pat Hill © 1996

May your points always meet
And your corners be square.
May your grain lines run straight
And there's fabric enough to spare.
May your stitches be even
And your miters be true.
May your batting lie flat
And your quilt win the blue.

And I will add, may you enjoy making quilts with constructed fabric.

Table of CONTENTS

Help! Don't be discouraged. The projects and ideas in this book give you wonderful new ways to use your scraps for quilts and wearable art.

Introduction

When I was writing this book, I thought of several wild and crazy titles for it. I want to share a few of them with you to help you understand what constructed fabric is all about.

Help, What Can I Do With My Scraps?

I Don't Want to Be the One Who Dies With the Most Fabric

subtitled: *My husband would then know the truth of what is under the bed, in the closet, in the pantry, in the…*

Quilts and Projects for Fabric Lovers

subtitled: *Waste not, want not*

Really Scrap Scrap Quilts

I think you can tell that I have a large collection of scraps. How about you? Do you have bags or boxes of fabric scraps that you don't know how to use, but hate to throw away?

If the answer is yes, read on. This book will provide you with the inspiration and skills to create unique and beautiful projects with your scraps.

I have been quilting seriously for ten years, so I have accumulated many boxes of strips, pieces, and scraps. They made nice stuffing material when my husband and I moved from Illinois to West Virginia but that didn't seem like a valid enough reason to keep them, so I began to study pictures of antique quilt collections and photographs of present day art quilts. I wanted to see if other quilters utilized their leftovers to make attractive quilts. I soon discovered that quilters, past and present, have sought to make use of their scraps and have done so in imaginative and successful ways.

I started sewing my scraps together to create new fabric. I call this fabric "constructed fabric" since it is constructed (made up) of all shapes and sizes of leftover fabric. I find that this new fabric is very versatile and can be used in many ways to make wonderful quilts and wearable art pieces.

This book introduces you to the exciting world of constructed fabric. You will become a "materials reduction/recycling engineer," and will be able to confidently proclaim, "Yes, I really do have a use for all these pieces of fabric."

Quilters of all skill levels can make and use constructed fabric. Experienced quilters will find constructed fabric a very creative technique, allowing for subtleties of color and design and beginners can make simple projects with attractive constructed fabric without analyzing and sorting their scraps.

Using constructed fabric also ties quilters to the historic tradition of quilt making, when fabric was expensive and every tiny piece was used or recycled. This technique appeals to our basic nature of waste not, want not.

Many of you probably think that all scraps are created equal. Not so. Chapter 1 reveals the differences between scraps and teaches you how to deal with quantities of scraps. Believe it or not, there are over 15 types of constructed fabric you can create and use in different quilt projects and you'll find samples of each of them.

Chapter 2 lets you in on secrets for quickly and enjoyably sewing your scraps into fabric. You'll discover how easy and rewarding it is to use constructed fabric in quilt blocks. Chapter 3 provides you with hints to make your design successful and includes more than 25 block designs.

Directions for 15 projects are provided in Chapter 4. These projects are easy to sew and offer a wide range of color schemes and themes. Finally, you'll find a descriptive photo gallery of constructed fabric projects in Chapter 5, including some very lovely wearable art pieces, to give you ideas and inspiration.

So, on your mark, get set, sew!

Joyce Mori

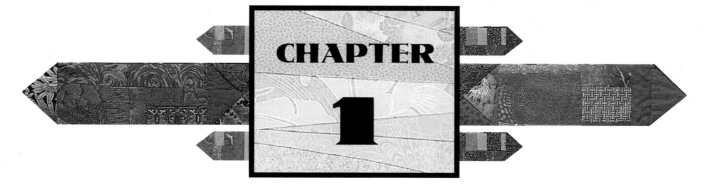

CHAPTER 1

Everything You Ever Wanted to Know About Constructed Fabric

Making constructed fabric is easy. You simply sew pieces of fabric—strips, scraps, specific geometric shapes—into a new piece of fabric. You then use this new piece of fabric to cut out the size and shape you need for your quilt project. Sew any leftover scraps of the constructed fabric to other scraps to produce another large piece of constructed fabric and cut out more pattern pieces.

Constructed fabric offers you a practical use for your leftover scraps, patches, and strips. But the real reason to make constructed fabric is because this new fabric is very interesting and attractive. By combining different types and colors of fabrics, you create a visually exciting and one-of-a-kind piece of new yardage.

Using constructed fabric in quilts and wearable art produces a much different and more exciting result than a single piece of commercial fabric. You can completely alter the look of a quilt block by sewing it from different types of constructed fabric. This is the same principle as changing the look of a quilt block by using striped fabric, large floral print fabric, tiny prints, etc. The opportunities for creative expression in your design are multiplied many times over when you sew and use constructed fabric.

The constructed fabric quilt blocks in this book are not sewn like a normal crazy quilt or string quilt fabric, where the fabric scraps are sewn onto a piece of foundation fabric or paper. As I sewed and cut out pieces of constructed fabric, I omitted the foundation because it added unneeded weight and an extra step to the process. Traditionalists might say the foundation is necessary to stabilize the bias edges of the random scraps, but if you follow the directions in this book you'll find that dealing with bias edges on constructed fabric is no more difficult than dealing with the bias edges of a triangle or irregular shape cut from regular fabric.

Because there's no foundation, the constructed fabric can be combined with regular commercial or hand-dyed fabrics and the weights of all the fabrics remain compatible. Combining a square of crazy patchwork sewn on a foundation fabric with a square of regular weight fabric is like combining a square of heavyweight flannel with organdy. The heavier fabric is likely to stretch the lighter fabric out of shape. I use constructed fabric for only parts of a design, so by omitting the foundation fabric, all the fabrics in the project are about the same weight. The one exception would be a constructed fabric type with many seams, which would be slightly heavier than a regular piece of fabric the same size. My quilts or wearable art items all make use of commercial fabrics as important parts of the design.

Where Do Scraps Come From?

If you don't have a scrap collection... My husband would probably tell you to call me, since he thinks I have far too much fabric! But a more realistic method is to work with your fabric stash. This method is the perfect excuse for straightening up and analyzing the fabric you have on hand. Take each piece of fabric in your stash and trim it up. You probably have uneven edges, curved edges, and so on. As you rotary cut a nice straight edge, you create scraps.

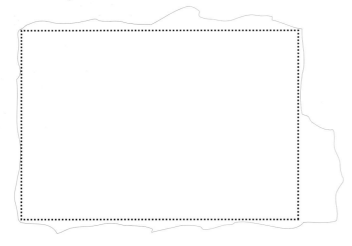

Figure 1-1
Trim the ragged edges.

Beg scraps from fellow quilters. Your quilt guild might schedule an exchange night where you can trade a fat quarter of fabric for a bag of scraps.

If you are new to quilting or a neatnik who threw out all your scraps, it is unlikely you have all the scraps you need for a project. This is especially true if you want to do a project using specific colors. Don't be afraid to put out the call to your friends that you need certain colors. Scraps are soon to become the quilter's currency for the 21st century!

Recognize Different Shapes of Scraps

As you look through a pile of scrap fabric, you will probably see some strips of uneven and even widths. There may be some specific geometric shapes—triangles, squares, rectangles—which represent unused pieces from previous quilt projects. You may even have some complete quilt blocks thrown into the mix, and lots of randomly shaped pieces (polygons).

Figure 1-2
Different types of scraps.

You might have a majority of one shape, with just a few of the others. If you do, study the specific projects in this book and select one that utilizes that shape to the best advantage.

Sorting Scraps

It can be overwhelming to sit in the midst of boxes or bags of scraps. You need to have some way to organize them.

There are several ways to sort scraps. The method you select may depend on the amount of time you have or the project you want to sew. If you are a mom with small children, get them to help you. The sorting process should be spaced out over several days and accommodate your work schedule. If you spend just a half hour each day, you will complete the job in no time and won't feel you have spent entire days on the sorting process with nothing to show for it.

Every few years I like to sort out my entire fabric stash. Normally I put small pieces of fabric (3″ x 12″, 8″ x 5″, etc.) into my regular assortment of fabrics, but they are really too small to be stored with the pieces 1/8 yard and larger. Pull these small pieces out and use them to make constructed fabric.

Before you begin sorting, assemble some containers—cardboard boxes, plastic storage bins, and so on—to sort the fabric into. A good size box is 12″ x 15″ x 7″. Cut off the tops of deep cardboard boxes so that you won't waste time digging around in the box to find scraps that are hidden below layers of other scraps. I don't recommend plastic bags because they are difficult to pull fabric out of when you start to sew.

Before you start to sort, read Steps 1 through 4 so you have an understanding of what you want to achieve. As you sort each category of fabric, put that fabric into a cardboard or plastic box. If you presort scraps into usable groups, it's easy for you to take that box filled with scraps to your sewing area and start to sew the fabric.

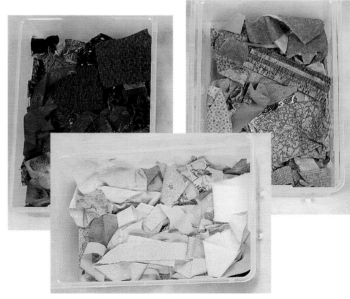

You need to sort your scraps by value—light, medium, and dark—before you begin sewing projects.

Step 1: Sort the scraps into two groups—solids and prints. You will notice projects in the book that use only solid colors, (A Taste of Amish, page 60). The bright colors make a very graphic and eye popping quilt. The majority of my scraps are not solid colors so I do not sort the solids down any farther than just solids. All of my solid scraps fit into one cardboard box.

Step 2: Further sort the prints into two or three groups: dark, light, and medium. You will notice that many of the projects make use of only the dark and light fabrics. Constructing such fabric is much easier if you have presorted your scraps into groups based on value, which simply means the lightness or darkness of the fabric.

However, value can be relative—a medium-value fabric placed next to a very dark fabric becomes a light-value in relationship to the dark fabric. This is especially important if you are creating a light-value background fabric for an appliqué design. You want the fabric to read as light-valued as possible to set off the appliqué motif. When you use fabrics in your light-value collection, set aside the slightly darker ones.

In some projects the value differences may be critical and a dark/medium fabric combined with dark/darks may spoil the look. At other times, an off-value fabric thrown into the mix might be just the eye-catching pop or variety you are looking for. You will make those decisions as you lay out your design and integrate commercial fabrics with the constructed fabric.

Consider purchasing a value finder device, such as the Ruby Beholder™ or Value Finder™ to help you better understand color value. A value finder is simply a piece of red or green plastic that takes the color out of a piece of fabric when you look through it, showing only the lightness or darkness of the color. It can be a great aid when you are sewing strips together and you want to make sure the block will read as all light, all medium, or all dark.

Step 3: If you have a lot of scraps and a lot of time, you can further sort your scraps into specific color groups. For instance, if you want a Christmas design, sort into red and green. Some of the Southwestern projects in this book are made of scraps sorted by rust and brown with accent pieces of purple and turquoise. If you like the Art Quilt project on page 48, sort out black and gray pieces.

Since you probably don't have large quantities of any one specific color group—red, purple, green, etc.—you can cut the tops off empty facial tissue boxes and sort each color or maybe two colors into each box.

Step 4: Many quilters dye their own fabric or use dyed and/or painted fabric in their quilts. If you have dyed fabric scraps, place them in a separate group. There are some projects in the book that make use of dyed fabric scraps, such as Gradations on page 57, Painted Stars on page 90, and the Sophisticated Gray vest on page 87.

Guidelines for Sewing Constructed Fabric

Carefully study the projects and pictures in this book to see what ideas you like best, then realistically assess your scraps to see if you have what you need to do such a project.

Because constructed fabric is an inventive and creative technique, I encourage you to experiment. I don't like to tell you that something won't work, because you may try it and be delighted with the results, but I will note some things that you should consider. Remember that rules are made to be broken, at least when it comes to being creative with your quilting.

• I avoid using knits for constructed fabric. I find that cotton and cotton/poly blends work best. I don't combine different weights and textures, but that doesn't mean it can't be done.

• Use only scraps from fabric that has been washed.

• Mixing strips of varying widths—some narrow, some wide—results in vivid and attractive blocks. A good example of this is Block #4 on page 11. Blocks from only even-width strips in one value aren't as interesting.

• Be careful when placing very light fabrics next to very dark fabrics. In some designs, a single light fabric scrap in the middle of dark ones will cause the eye to focus on the light scrap and destroy the continuity of the piece. This also happens if a dark fabric that has a small amount of light color as part of the pattern is added to an otherwise all dark piece. The eye is drawn to the light color and you lose the feeling of a dark block.

Of course, adding some light pieces to dark pieces can add interest to a block, so you'll need to evaluate each design individually. Surrounding a light piece with dark and light pieces can create the illusion of a planned skewed log cabin block, as shown in Block #17 on page 14. Depending on the project, this can be quite effective.

• Balance the size of the fabric pieces. Don't combine one very wide strip with tiny random pieces in the same block because everything will appear out of proportion.

It is also important to have the scale of the scrap pieces in proportion to the project template. There is a completely different effect when a 3″ square is made from four scraps of fabric (Fig. 1-3) than when a 3″ square is made from many scrap pieces (Fig. 1-4).

Figure 1-4
A square with many pieces.

You now know about the variety of scraps you might have in your collection and you have seen examples of how the scraps can be combined. In Chapter 2 you sit down and begin to sew. The fun begins.

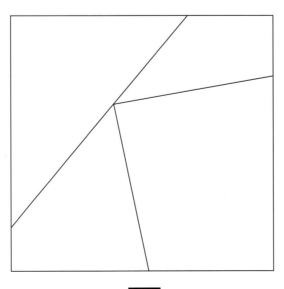

Figure 1-3
A square with a small number of pieces.

Constructed Fabric Blocks

To help you better understand the wide variety of constructed fabric it is possible to make, I have sewn a series of six-inch square blocks using a variety of constructed fabric types. If you look carefully at these blocks and read the description that accompanies each, you will understand the nature of constructed fabric.

Even though you will probably make sections rather than blocks of constructed fabric, I chose this format to show the relationship between the size of pieces in a block, the number of pieces in a block, and the overall look of the fabric. You will quickly see that not all constructed fabric is the same and that the types of fabric you sew together will influence the way your quilt project will look.

When I think of a section of constructed fabric as part of a quilt design, I see it as adding visual variety to the quilt. The constructed area looks as if complex piecing went into its construction and the wide variety of colors and/or patterns give it visual punch.

When working with strips, notice the two different types: even-width strips that are the same width along the entire length of the strip, whether it's one inch, two inches, etc.; and uneven-width strips that taper from wide to narrow along the length.

Block #1 Even-width strips cut all the same width

The strips in this quilt are dark print fabrics. While there is nothing wrong with this block, it is simply basic strip piecing and does not allow you to take advantage of the creative potential of your scraps.

Figure 1-5
An uneven width strip (top) and an even width strip.

Block #2 Dark print even-width strips cut different widths

These dark colored even-width strips are cut in different widths, sewn together and then cut into a block. This is basically strip piecing except you use leftover strips with no color considerations except in regard to dark and light values. The fabrics are all prints. Varying the widths adds more interest to the block.

Block #3 Dyed even-width strips cut different widths

These even-width strips are from dyed fabrics that have been cut different widths. The fabrics are a mix of solid colors and slightly mottled colors. Even though it is the same block type as #2, it looks different because of the fabric.

Block #4   Uneven-width strips

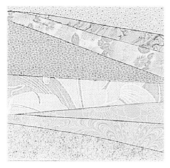

This light-value block is made from strips of uneven width and you can see how this adds interest to the block. Remember that you can often use the wrong side of a piece of fabric to achieve a lighter value and thus stretch your scrap supply.

Block #5   Solid colors

The pieces in this block are mostly rectangles sewn together in medium to dark value ranges. The block is cut out on an angle so the pieces appear more random in size and shape.

Block #6   Dyed crazy quilt

The randomly shaped pieces are from medium-value dyed fabrics in solid, multicolor, and mottled colors.

Block #7   One color crazy quilt

Only green-tone scraps, prints, and solids are used for this block, which makes it perfect for Christmas quilt projects. The fabric includes strips and random pieces in values from medium to dark. Visually this is a very interesting block.

Block #8   Dark print crazy quilt

This block consists of dark and dark/medium-value print fabrics of random shapes and strip pieces. The slight differences in value add interest to the overall appearance. Notice the range of individual colors used.

Block #9   Light print crazy quilt

This is the same type as block #8 except the fabrics are all light-value. Obviously, you could use medium-value fabrics as well. The Purple Pinwheel on page 38 shows how effective such fabrics can be in a quilt. The light-value crazy quilt type is also very useful as a background for an appliqué design.

Block #10 Dark print and solid crazy quilt

This is the same type block as #8 and #9 except that print and solid fabrics are combined, which stretches your fabric scrap supply and makes the block more colorful. This block could be called the "quilter's fabric stew." In a single color block, such as block #7, using solid fabrics with prints can reinforce the color because print fabrics do not always read as a single color. Adding the solid color pieces emphasizes the color you wish to showcase in the print fabrics.

Block #11 Diagonals

This block features uneven-width strips in both dark and light values. The light-value strips are wider so the dark-value strips appear to slash across the light background. This block emphasizes directional line. The careful placement of such a block can focus the viewer's eye toward something else.

Notice that one of the light diagonal strips

was pieced. Sewing small scraps of the same value together to create a longer strip helps you make use of smaller pieces in your scrap collection.

Block #12 Slashing block

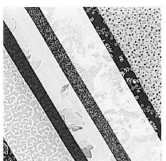

This block features even-width strips with alternating dark and light values. The dark strips are narrow and the light strips are wide. This block could be considered a more formal approach to the Diagonals block. The block is cut on a diagonal, but not at an exact 45 degree angle. The square template is placed so the lines of the strips are at some type of diagonal, which gives the block visual interest.

Block #13 Alternating wedges

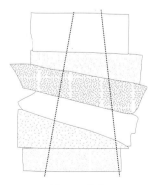

Figure 1-6
Cutting a row of strips.

This block is made of separate light and dark components, each sewn separately. A long strip of light fabric strips, uneven and even width, are sewn together. The strip is trimmed on two edges at a slight angle to true perpendicular.

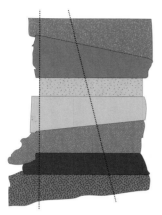

Figure 1-7
Cutting a wedge section from dark strips.

A set of dark strips is also sewn and two sides are trimmed straight.

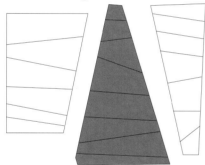

Figure 1-8

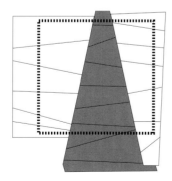

Figure 1-9
Sewing the wedges together and cutting a block from them.

A dark wedge unit is sewn between two light wedge units.

The block is cut to size. Remaining wedge sections can be used as the basis for succeeding blocks.

Block #14 Gradation

This block is sewn with strips of uneven and even widths within the blue color family. As you sew, start with light strips and gradually add darker and darker strips. Not every strip needs to be pieced in a gradated sequence. Some strips can be left as a whole. Gradations on page 57 is an example of this type of constructed fabric sewn in a carefully planned way and without the black spacing strips.

Block #15 Tiny pieces

This block uses only relatively small size scraps. Obviously, this requires a lot more sewing, i.e. seams in a block, but it also makes for a very colorful block and allows you to use up a lot more scraps. Such pieces of constructed fabric are best used in quilt projects with large size templates.

Block #16 Art quilt

I call this an art quilt block because high key (bright) solid fabrics are combined with black and white prints. This nontraditional block makes a vivid visual impact.

Block #17 Unconventional log cabin

This block features a center scrap with four sides. The lopsided scrap center is neither a perfect square nor rectangle, which gives the block its unconventional appearance. Sew the block like any log cabin by adding a strip to one side, trimming it on each end, and then adding a strip on the next side and so on. When enough strips have been added around the center, the block is trimmed to size. Using uneven-width strips adds to the unconventional but attractive appearance of this traditional quilt block.

Block #18 Shadings

As you look at this block, notice that it shades from dark to medium to light. You could also shade in only two values—light to medium, dark to medium, or light to dark.

Special Blocks: Influences

These blocks are my tribute to various quilters who have used something like constructed fabric in their quilts. The blocks are not meant to copy their work but are meant to emphasize some aspect of their quilts by translating it into my ideas for constructed fabric. Keep in mind that these quilters carefully select each piece of fabric and often use templates for each of the crazy piece shapes. I want to promote a freer, looser approach to the selection of fabrics and piecing. These ideas are a little more difficult to piece so don't try them until you have played around with the general idea of constructed fabric.

Block #19 Anna Williams

Anna has a wonderful intuitive skill to combine bright, wild, and unconnected colors together to create visually spectacular quilts. The quilt I used for inspiration—A Li'l Bit Crazy Two—seems to be based on a rectangular grid. I wanted to use a square format to keep all the constructed block ideas the same, but it is the diagonal lines across the block that intrigued me. Anna's work reminds me of the antique string pieced quilts I have seen in books and magazines.

Block #20 Jan Meyers Newberry

Jan has used some crazy patchwork in her quilts. My adaptation of her work is to use dyed fabrics, which are Jan's specialty, in larger size pieces. We often find ourselves with larger pieces of fabric which we hate to cut up. Certainly if you use three to six pieces of fabric per block, you reduce your sewing time.

Sew your constructed fabric of larger sized scraps, then cut the pattern pieces as usual from this fabric. If you select one light-value piece of fabric, you'll have a definite contrast with the other pieces of the block and the design will appear to have been deliberately cut and pieced with individual templates. This is really an improvised block and no two will ever be the same because of the different shapes of the pieces.

Block #21 Judith Larzelere

Judith works with strip piecing techniques and one thing that intrigues me about her work is her use of very tiny spots of color in narrow strips. Since you probably have some very small pieces of fabric, this block adaptation is something to consider. You can also use Seminole strip piecing, as I did for my example, to create the central area of tiny dashes of color and you can use more than one strip of color spots in a block.

Block #22 Dorle Stern-Straeter

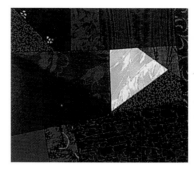

Dorle's crazy quilts seem to have a sparkle of color in them. She carefully plans her quilts and the use of light and dark values. I find the surprise appearance of a touch of color throughout the quilt to be a wonderful idea. I call this block type "Sparkle" because it has a touch of a very contrasting color in it.

Block #23 Paul Klee

The inspiration for this block comes from Paul Klee's painting, *The Way to the Citadel*. As I stood in the art museum studying the painting, one particular feature caught my eye—a rectangle enclosed within a picture frame, mitered corner border, surrounded by all manner of odd-shaped geometric designs.

For my constructed fabric block, I sewed two triangles together to form a square and framed it with a mitered corner border. I enclosed this with various strips and pieces. Remember that constructed fabric is made from scraps, so my center square is not truly square because the triangles were not the same size. I sewed the mitered borders without measuring, so they are not perfect, but it is the essence of the idea I wanted to duplicate. Setting the mitered corner unit off center creates even more interest in the block.

Chapter 2

Sewing Constructed Fabric

The instructions for the project you choose will tell you what type of constructed fabric to sew and this is where the fun begins. Sewing constructed fabric isn't difficult, in fact it can even be a therapeutic form of relaxation. No matter how hectic life around me becomes, I find it difficult to go a day without sitting down at the sewing machine and sewing a few seams. If I don't want to take the time to cut out pieces or think about a pattern, I dig into a scrap box and start sewing pieces together. The only problem is that I hate to stop sewing…there's always one more piece I would like to add to finish off a section of fabric.

You don't need to sew an entire piece of usable constructed fabric at one time. I often sew a couple scraps together when I am finishing off my regular chain sewing for another quilt project. I sew constructed fabric while I'm waiting for a phone call or for a friend to come over. Soon I have enough constructed fabric to start a project.

Your quilting group might enjoy a night program of sewing constructed fabric as a fun change of pace. If you are sewing constructed fabric during a workshop you will soon see how much fun it is to talk, joke, and sew with friends. You can share a pizza, trade scraps, and get lots of ideas from the color combinations and patterns that result when different quilters use their stashes of fabric scraps to make "new" fabric.

Preparation

If you are going to sit down to sew large pieces of constructed fabric, you'll need to make a few preparations. If you want to maintain your momentum after you start, load a new spool of thread and a full bobbin on the machine before you begin to sew. However, sewing constructed fabric is a great way to use up ugly thread colors or spools with only small amounts of thread left on them.

Have several bobbins filled and ready for use and make sure you have oiled and serviced your machine according to the directions. You will be doing a lot of sewing so treat your machine accordingly. This is a good time to put in a sharp new needle. Sewing authorities recommend that you replace a needle after eight hours of use, but most of us tend to sew with a needle until it breaks.

In addition to your sewing machine, you will need an iron and ironing board and a rotary cutter and plastic ruler.

Keep the box of scraps in a handy spot on the floor beside your machine so you can reach in and pull out scraps as needed.

Starting to Sew

Cut any selvages off the scraps. The selvage is usually tighter than the main piece of fabric and can distort the section of constructed fabric if you use it.

To streamline the process of sewing scraps, practice chain sewing. This allows you to sew on many separate groups of pieces at once.

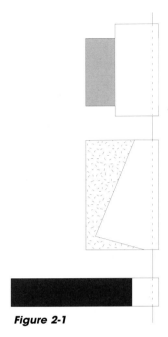

Figure 2-1

Select two scraps and sew them together. Do not cut the thread. Sew two more scraps and so on. Continue until you have a chain of sewn scraps.

Stop and cut the sections of scraps apart. At this point you can proceed by sewing some of these two scrap units together or by adding a single scrap to a two scrap unit. You only need to finger press a seam to the side. You decide where to add pieces by noting how the scraps fit together.

Below are some drawings that illustrate types of scraps and how they might be joined together. Look at the entire process as solving a puzzle, where you must select the right pieces to fit the raw edge.

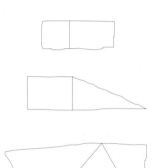

Figure 2-2
Different ways to sew pieces together.

Trouble-shooting Tips

• If you have a strip of tiny pieces sewn together, attach a regular strip to it rather than another strip of constructed fabric (Fig. 2-3). This reduces the excess bulk of many seams being joined together and adds interest to the

fabric by adding a counterpoint to the tiny pieces.

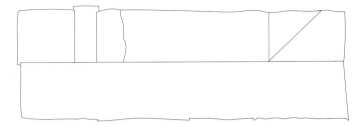

Figure 2-3
Attach a strip of tiny pieces to a plain strip.

• Don't throw away rounded edge pieces. You can attach a rounded edge scrap to straight edge pieces by using one of the methods shown below.

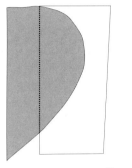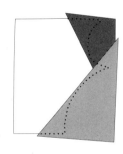

Figure 2-4
Two ways to attach a rounded edge piece to a straight edge piece.

• If you have a piece with a sharp acute angle on one edge, attach a triangle shape to it.

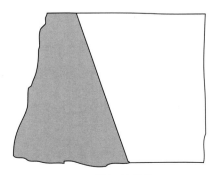

Figure 2-5
Attach a triangle to a piece with a sharp acute angle.

• If you have a piece with a jagged edge,

don't try to sew another piece to it along the jagged edge. You'll end up with a bowed seam that will not press flat. Instead, trim the jagged edge and attach your other strip to that straight edge.

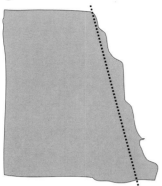

Figure 2-6
Trim a jagged edge before trying to attach another piece of fabric.

• Try to vary the shape of the scraps in a piece. Don't have all triangles or even strips. Study the blocks on pages 10-15 for examples of using different shapes in pieces.

• If you add a piece of fabric that is too light, too dark, or does not blend with the other pieces, cut it out. It won't look any better as time goes by and will ruin the effect of your constructed fabric pattern pieces.

This is especially important when you are sewing a blended value piece of constructed fabric—for example, a piece that should read all dark. However, the Squares: Solid and Hollow quilt on page 54 shows constructed fabric where light pieces are sewn onto dark pieces and the squares do not read as all dark. In this case, the edges of the squares are blurred and the squares do not look continuous. Using non-blended fabrics in the design adds an element of spontaneity. The choice is yours, depending on how you want the design to look.

• If you're short of light- or medium-value scraps, you may be able to use the wrong side of the fabric, which often has more subtle coloring and texture.

• If you have only large scraps, sew them together, then cut up this sewn fabric into several sections. Resew the parts together for a piece with more visual texture. You may have to add some additional scraps and trim up the piece of fabric.

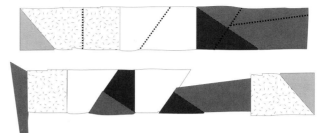

Figures 2-7 and 2-8
Consider cutting these larger pieces along the dotted lines and then resew the units back together in a different way.

• Keep the size of your scraps in proportion to the quilt pattern templates. You will need to sort the right size scraps before beginning to sew.

For example, if you sew a piece of constructed fabric from scraps that are 3″ or 4″ square and then cut out 3″ triangles, it's unlikely that you will have any seam line in the pattern piece and it won't look at all like a piece of constructed fabric.

If you have only large scraps, select a quilt project with larger pattern pieces or follow the method noted above where you sew your scraps together, cut them up and resew them.

• Don't worry if two triangles don't fit together exactly. Just sew them together and trim the section up later. Sewing constructed fabric is not a meticulous fitting job. It's a technique where you can cut off tips of triangles and have lopsided squares, etc. These odd features make the fabric unique and interesting.

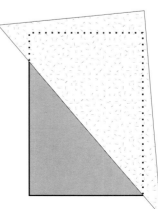

Figure 2-9
Sew two different size triangles together and then trim them into perhaps a rectangle shape.

• Don't stretch pieces to fit a space. You are dealing with many bias edges so you don't want to pull scraps out of shape. Lay the pieces on top of one another, sew without pulling, and trim it later.

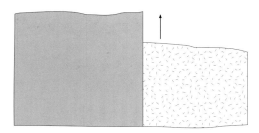

Figure 2-10
Don't try to stretch the one side of the small rectangle to fit the side of the larger rectangle.

• If you are sewing a bias strip, it helps to encase it between strips with non-bias edges or between a strip of constructed fabric without a definite bias edge.

Time to Iron

There is no hard and fast rule about when to iron. My general approach is to head off to the ironing board when I have about four scrap pieces sewn together. I iron the piece flat, ironing the seams toward the darker color if possible.

When you lay a piece of constructed fabric on the ironing board, it has a tendency to lie in the direction its seams should be pressed. It's best to iron the seams toward the darkest fabric to hide the seam allowance, but you won't always be able to do this because you must always iron the seams in the direction that most reduces the bulk and allows the fabric to lie as flat as possible. For example, when you iron a piece with a large number of seams, iron them flat, not back under themselves.

If I have a glaringly uneven edge along one part of this patchwork piece, I trim it with a rotary cutter so it will be easy to fit more scraps along it (see Figs. 2-11 and 2-12).

If you intend to quilt on the piece of constructed fabric, determine what type of quilting you want to do before you iron your

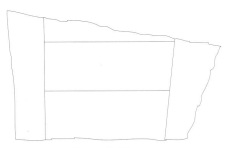

Figure 2-11
The edges on this piece are even enough to be left untrimmed.

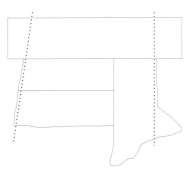

Figure 2-12
The uneven edges on this piece require trimming on the dotted lines.

seam allowances open or in either direction. If you plan to hand-quilt a project with constructed fabric in it, you will probably quilt in the ditch around the piece, so carefully press your seams to one side to reduce the bulk on one side of the ditch. Quilting in the ditch around each patch outlines the patches and raises them up or puffs them slightly above the surface of the quilt.

If you want to quilt in the constructed fabric, press the seams open. When I quilt across constructed fabric, I use pieces sewn with large size scraps and don't worry if my quilting stitches are tiny or not. However, keep in mind that quilting stitches aren't likely to show up in a block with a lot of print pieces.

Completed Fabric

Keep sewing on your pieces of constructed fabric until you have a piece of fabric *approxi-*

mately 12" x 12". Sit down at your sewing machine any time you have a few extra moments in your day. Make all kinds of constructed fabric. Keep your pieces of constructed fabric in a box separate from your scraps, so that when you're ready to make one of the projects or to design a project for yourself, you can pull out the pieces and see what type of fabric you have to work with.

As quilters you are probably used to thinking in terms of fat quarters (18" x 22"), but with constructed fabric the units probably won't ever be as large as a fat quarter. If you need a larger piece, you can sew completed squares together. It takes four 12" square pieces to equal a fat quarter.

You can certainly make your piece of fabric larger than 12" square but don't make it smaller. You want a piece of constructed fabric large enough to cut a number of pattern pieces from and large enough to allow you to selectively place your template when you cut out a pattern piece.

You will want to have three or four pieces that are approximately 12" square before you begin to work on the projects in the book. This may or may not be enough fabric to finish a project, depending on the project, so be prepared to sew more constructed fabric to complete a project.

You can often use the trimmings left from these first pieces of constructed fabric to make more. Don't reuse strips that are less than ½" wide or pieces with a large number of seams. For example, if you have a scrap that is 1" by 5" made up of nine or more scraps, discard it. There are just too many seams to use it again in constructed fabric.

← 1" →

5"

**Figure 2-13
This scrap is not suitable to be used as part of an additional piece of constructed fabric.**

Block #15, Tiny Pieces on page 13 is an exception to this rule. In this case, select a pattern piece that is large enough so that there won't be many additional seams when joining it to other pieces.

Placing the Template

Scraps that have been sewn into pieces of constructed fabric.

The three pieces of constructed fabric shown in the photo are ready to be cut into pattern templates. To start, I usually square up the edge against which I am going to line up the template.

The directions for the projects in this book list the total amount of fabric for each pattern piece. This allows you to use regular fabric in place of constructed fabric if you wish. Therefore, when the fabric requirements list ½ yard of constructed fabric, this means a number of smaller pieces (12" x 12", 12" x 14", 10" x 15", etc.), not the full ½ yard amount. It will take approximately six such pieces to equal ½ yard. You can use constructed fabric for any template as long as the template piece is not too small. You don't want to use constructed fabric in a 2″ square or triangle or for anything smaller.

Sew the pieces of constructed fabric larger than what you will need. For example, if you need a 6″ square of constructed fabric, sew a piece at least 8″ square. This allows you to move the template to the best position on the fabric. Use a clear plastic template to determine the best placement of the pattern piece on the constructed fabric. This is especially important when you want to emphasize the diagonal lines of certain types of constructed fabric (see Slashing Squares on page 42 and Diagonals on page 51).

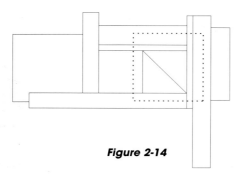

Figure 2-14

Move the template to the best position on the fabric.

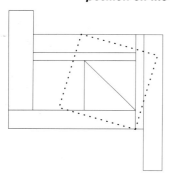

Figure 2-15

The piece of constructed fabric must also be large enough to allow you to position the template so that the sewing line, which is ¼″ inside the cutting line, is not along a seam line or in the seam allowance of the constructed fabric. This would be impossible to sew. Reposition the template so any major seam line on the constructed fabric is at least ¾″ from the edge of the template.

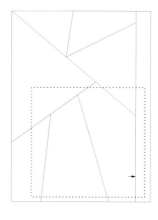

**Figure 2-16
Don't place the square template in this position. The seam line on the constructed fabric (marked with an arrow) would be too close to the sewing line for square.**

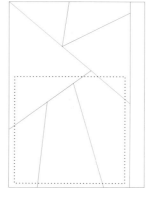

**Figure 2-17
This is a better placement for the template.**

Don't spend a great deal of time placing a template on the fabric. You can always cut the fabric and add another strip to it later or sew it onto another set of scraps if you have a problem with seams.

When you look at your scraps and at the finished projects in this book, it's natural to be excited and eager to make up many types of constructed fabric all at once. You can do that, but I suggest you limit yourself to sewing a few very basic forms of constructed fabric at first. This way, you will quickly and easily learn the technique and will have usable fabric. For your initial project, don't concern yourself with design options.

The Star Block:
A Good Starter Project

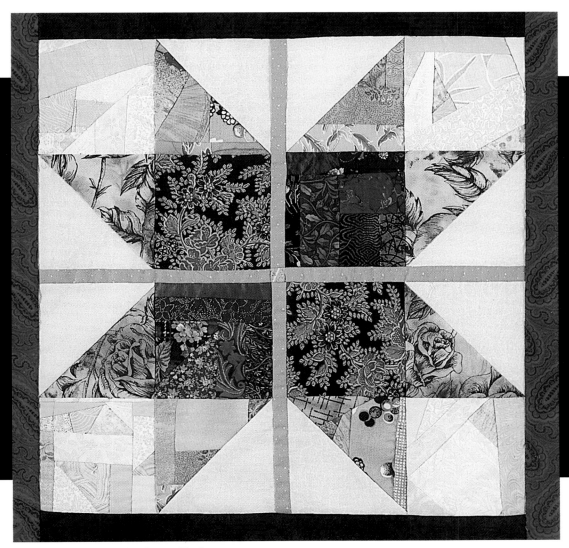

Designed and sewn by Joyce Mori.

After you've sorted your scraps according to solids/prints and dark/light/medium as suggested in Chapter 1, you're ready to get down to business. Here is a quick and easy first project for you to sew. You will make a small quilt block which you can use as a pillow top or the center panel of a table runner. By adding more borders, you can create a small wall quilt, or you can sew three more blocks and make a large wall quilt.

Name of Quilt: Star Block
Finished Size: 18½" x 18½"
Skill Level: Beginner
Line Drawing on page 93

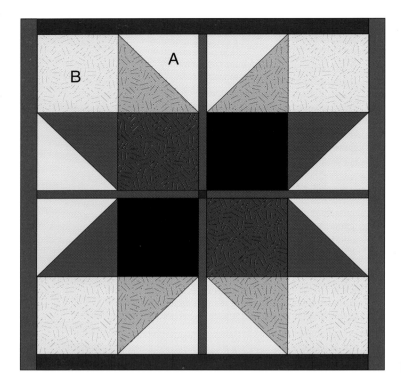

Light Value Constructed

Light Value

Medium Value Constructed

Medium Value

Dark Value Constructed

Dark Value *(Three colors)*

Figure 2-18

Constructed Fabric Requirements

• 10" square of light-value constructed fabric. Use solids and prints and combine strips and pieces. The wrong side of some fabrics can be used for light values.

• 5" x 10" piece of dark-value constructed fabric. Use solids and prints and whatever shape scrap you have on hand.

• 5" x 11" piece of medium-value constructed fabric. Combine solids and prints and whatever strips or shapes you have on hand. You can sometimes use the wrong side of dark fabrics for medium-value pieces.

Non-constructed Fabric Requirements

• 11" square of light fabric

• 5" x 11" piece of medium fabric

• 5" x 10" piece of dark fabric

• 4 pieces of medium fabric 1" x 9" for sashing between quarters

• 2 strips of dark fabric 1½" x 20" for side borders

• 2 strips of a different dark fabric 1½" x 22" for top and bottom borders

• 1" x 1" square of medium fabric for center square

Cutting Chart

Template A (from page 101)

• 4 constructed medium-value

• 4 non-constructed medium

• 8 non-constructed light

Template B (from page 103)

• 4 constructed light-value

• 2 constructed dark-value

• 2 non-constructed dark

Making the Quilt

The Star Block is made of four quarter blocks joined by sashing strips and a small center square. Each quarter block is composed of four triangles (Template A) and two squares (Template B). The cutting chart details the fabric types and the diagram shows you how to place them.

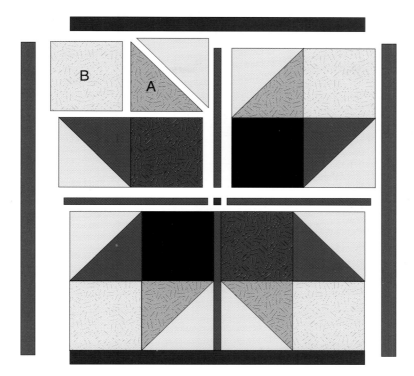

Figure 2-19

1. Refer to the diagram and sew two Template As (one medium constructed, one non-constructed light) together to form a square. Sew two more Template As (one non-constructed medium, one non-constructed light) to form a second square. Refer to the diagram and sew these two squares to two Template B squares to form a quarter block. Make four quarter blocks.

2. Sew two of the quarter block units together with a sashing strip to form a half. Repeat.

3. Sew the small center square between two sashing strips to form a long strip. Sew the two halves together with this strip between them.

4. Sew on the top and bottom border pieces first, then complete the quilt top by sewing on the side border pieces.

Quilting

1. Assemble the quilt top, batting, and backing together in a quilt sandwich. Quilt as desired.

2. Bind and label your quilt.

Doing this project shows you how fun and rewarding it is to sew with constructed fabric. The Star Block you created is very attractive, truly one-of-a-kind, and has a great deal more visual personality than one made with non-constructed fabrics.

Chapter 3

Designing With Constructed Fabric

Selecting a Design

Most quilt patterns can be used for constructed fabric designs, but there are two major design considerations to remember. First, this is not a technique for miniatures. You are already working with small pieces so don't cut 1″ patterns out of them. I prefer to work with designs that include 3″ or larger (finished size) triangles and squares.

Secondly, do not select a design with lots of seams, such as an eight-pointed star. The star design begins with eight seams and if you cut the points from constructed fabric, you will have even more seams at the point, which will be much too bulky. If you want to do a design with many points meeting, you'll need to carefully place the pattern template with the narrow point on a part of the fabric without any additional seams or alternate a constructed fabric star point with a non-constructed one.

The diagrams that follow show block drawings that are suitable for constructed fabric designs. The constructed fabric appears as patterned pieces and non-constructed fabric appears as solid pieces.

Keep in mind that if you make a nine block wall quilt of one design, such as the Greek Cross on page 28, you can alternate a block that features constructed fabric with a block that uses only commercial or regular fabrics. To maintain balance in the quilt design, use the same values and/or colors in both the non-constructed and constructed blocks. This is a good method for first projects because you can quickly sew the small amount of constructed fabric needed.

Alternating constructed and non-constructed pieces also works well with the Windmill design on page 29. Two of the spokes are of constructed fabric and the other two are of regular fabric. This helps stretch your constructed fabric supply. Of course, if you have large quantities of scraps and are sewing lots of constructed fabric, you can make all four spokes with constructed fabric.

When you look at any of the designs, remember that you can use as much or as little constructed fabric as you choose. Plan your design so the constructed fabric is the focus of the quilt. I never use constructed fabric for an entire quilt—it would take too long to make and would probably weigh twice as much as a regular quilt because of all the seams.

If you like to do appliqué work, you'll find that constructed fabric makes a wonderful background. To see examples of this, turn to Blue Swirls on page 91 and Tulip Quilts on pages 89-90. In Tulip Quilts, the constructed fabric becomes part of the appliqué design.

For your convenience, line drawings of all the projects in the book appear in Appendix A which begins on page 92. Make copies of the ones you like and experiment with color and where to use constructed fabric. Don't underestimate your own creative intuition.

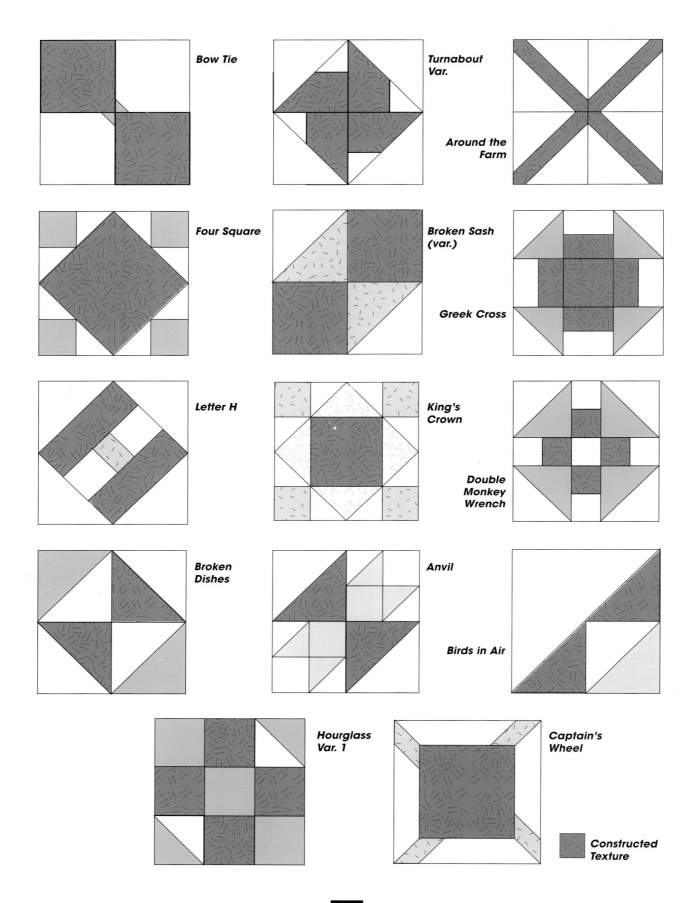

Bow Tie

Turnabout Var.

Around the Farm

Four Square

Broken Sash (var.)

Greek Cross

Letter H

King's Crown

Double Monkey Wrench

Broken Dishes

Anvil

Birds in Air

Hourglass Var. 1

Captain's Wheel

Constructed Texture

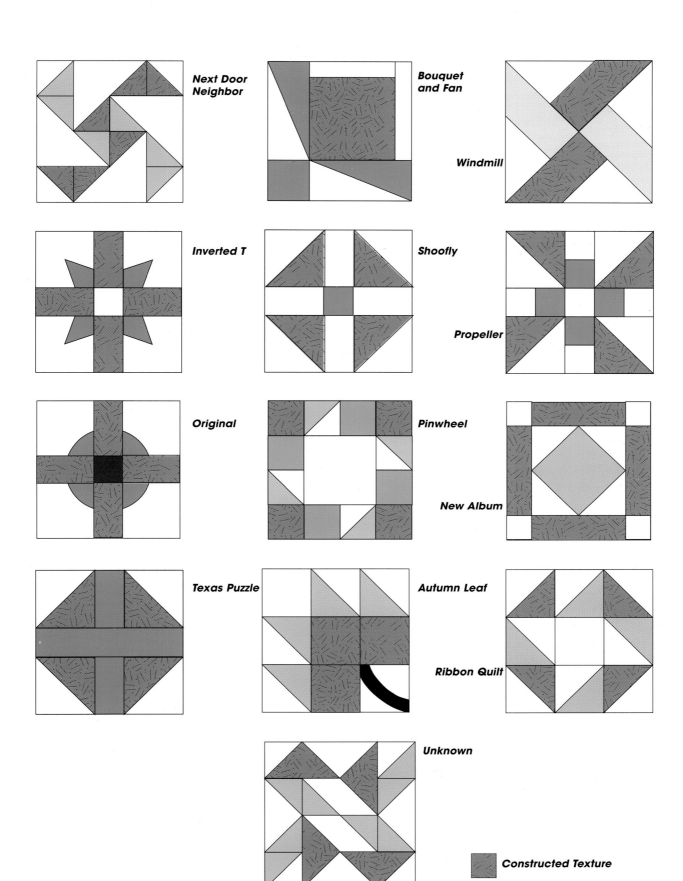

Next Door
Neighbor

Bouquet
and Fan

Windmill

Inverted T

Shoofly

Propeller

Original

Pinwheel

New Album

Texas Puzzle

Autumn Leaf

Ribbon Quilt

Unknown

Constructed Texture

One Design— Many Looks

You've seen some of the different types of constructed fabric you can sew. Now let's see what happens when you cut up these constructed fabric pieces and sew them in a specific geometric shape. You will quickly see that different types of constructed fabric look different in the same design.

Study this set of ten blocks very carefully. They will be a source of inspiration for your future projects. All the blocks are made from the same templates—a 4″ square and a 4″ triangle. The squares and triangles are put together in different ways and are colored in different ways in terms of light, dark, and medium value. This is an easy block to cut out and sew and you might consider it for an entire project. There are innumerable ways the block can be put together and colored.

Not all types of constructed fabric discussed in Chapter 1 are used in these blocks. This is just a sampling to provide you with a variety of examples. Study the different types of constructed fabric and the effects each creates in the block. These blocks illustrate the creative and varied results you can achieve with constructed fabric.

Diagonals

This block uses Diagonals constructed fabric (Block #11, page 12). However, the fabric is really scraps of diagonal fabric that have been sewn together. Some of the directional impact of the true constructed fabric is lost, but the light and dark strips make for a very exciting center star design. The red in the outside triangles complements the red strips in the diagonal scraps and brings the entire design together. The light green swirl further enhances the design and nicely complements the red.

Crazy quilt, specific color

When seen at a distance, the black constructed fabric appears as a single piece of fabric rather than constructed fabric because all the blacks are very dark. The center star is not emphasized in this block because it is created with a medium-value print with black and pale rose/peach. When you select a print with several colors you can tie everything together by using constructed fabric of one of the colors and a background of another.

Tiny pieces

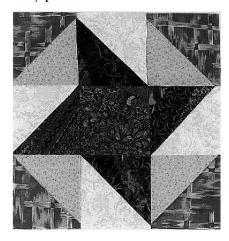

The medium-value center star is made from sections of constructed fabric sewn of tiny pieces (Block #15, page 13). It looks like a lovely multicolored print. The dark print is a darker value of one of the colors found in the constructed fabric.

Different widths, even-cut strips

The center star is made from constructed fabric as shown in Block #2 on page 10. In this piece, the edge of the template is not lined up parallel to any strip and the pieces are cut out at an angle to the strips. The detail of the separate strips comes into focus as you get closer to the piece. Cutting the strips at an angle makes the design more interesting.

Crazy quilt, dyed fabric

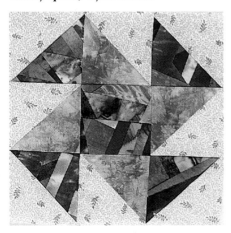

All types of dyed and painted fabrics are used to make the constructed fabric in Block #6 on page 11. There are areas of light, dark, and medium fabrics and almost every color of

the rainbow is included. A mottled dyed fabric is used for the center star. This example shows how randomly selected fabrics can be effectively sewn together to make a piece of attractive constructed fabric.

Crazy quilt, specific color group

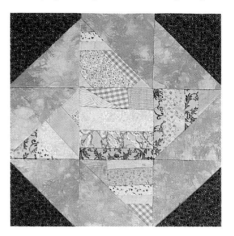

Light blue fabrics in strips and random shapes make up this constructed fabric (Block #7, page 11). The dark blue corners and middle of medium-value orange (blue's complementary color) give this block a cool calming look.

Solid colors

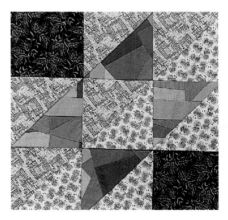

Compare this block with the Amish projects in this book. A gray/white print sets off the solid colored constructed fabric (Block #5, page 11) instead of the black used in the Amish projects and two different gray prints make up the background, one slightly lighter than the other. This block appears less frenetic than it would if a black background was used, but it is still very lively looking. Notice the center star is eliminated when the block is put together this way.

Crazy quilt, light print

The very light crazy print constructed fabric (Block #9, page 11) really sets off the dark brown commercial print and makes a more interesting background than would a single print piece of fabric. A lovely brown and rust print with gold accents is used in the corners. This block illustrates the versatility of light-value constructed fabric and how well elegant fabrics blend with constructed fabrics.

Crazy quilt, dark print

The constructed fabric (Block #8, page 11) is made of light/dark and dark/medium fabrics. Several of the fabrics are very colorful prints. I used a gold print for the center to give the block a bright, almost Mexican flavor. The touches of gold in the prints of the constructed fabric help to coordinate the overall appearance.

Slashing

The dark star in this block stands out against the light background fabrics. Adding to the emphasis of the star design is the use of constructed fabric type #11 (Diagonals) in the four square corners of the block. The directional nature of the constructed fabric serves to reinforce the focus on the points of the star.

You could create a sampler quilt of constructed fabric with these nine basic patch blocks, using all dark or all light fabrics sewn in the different types of constructed fabric. To develop more types of constructed fabric, organize a "constructed fabric exchange" at your guild, much like an exchange of commercial fabrics for charm quilts. Constructed fabric is really lots of fun to work with, so use these ideas as a springboard for your own creative adaptations.

Experimenting With Design

Some of the constructed fabric types pictured in Chapter 1 are really treated as a form of yardage that features blended value—light, medium, or dark—or blended color—varieties of blue, for example.

However, some of the constructed fabric types such as Wedges, Slashing block, Shadings, Diagonals, Gradation, and the Influences can be sewn and treated as separate pieced blocks. When sewn and trimmed to a shape, the fabric looks like a block of several planned pieces that have been drawn from templates and sewn together. They are truly "template free" quilt blocks.

You may want to devise quilt designs that emphasize and make use of the inherent lines and value changes of these forms of constructed fabric. How do you proceed?

First, trace some block versions of the constructed fabric types from Chapter 1 and make four to nine copies of each block. Then arrange these blocks in a four-block or nine-block format. You can arrange the blocks so they touch each other, are separated by a plain square, or are separated by a sashing strip. Study Slashing Squares (page 42), Diagonals (page 51), and A Taste of Amish, Triangles (page 90) to see some examples.

Rotate the blocks to change the directional lines or shading. The lines can go in every direction, all in the same direction, or pointing toward the center.

Figures 3-2 through 3-5 show how this might be done with the Alternating wedges type of constructed fabric (Block #13, page 12). You could also add plain blocks in this arrangement or add sashing strips.

When you find an arrangement you like, glue the photocopied blocks on a piece of paper and use this as the piecing diagram to complete your quilt.

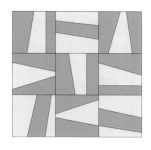

Figure 3-2

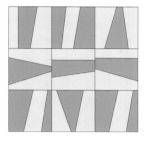

Figure 3-3

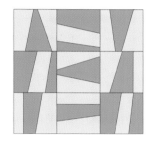

Figure 3-4

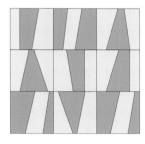

Figure 3-5

Some Final Notes

Just because you are making constructed fabric from leftover scraps doesn't mean you should not take your quilt design seriously. This is a very creative technique. You must determine where to use the constructed fabric, what type of constructed fabric to sew, and which commercial or dyed fabric to combine with the constructed fabric. Select your coordinating fabrics as carefully as you would select the fabrics to use in any quilt top or garment.

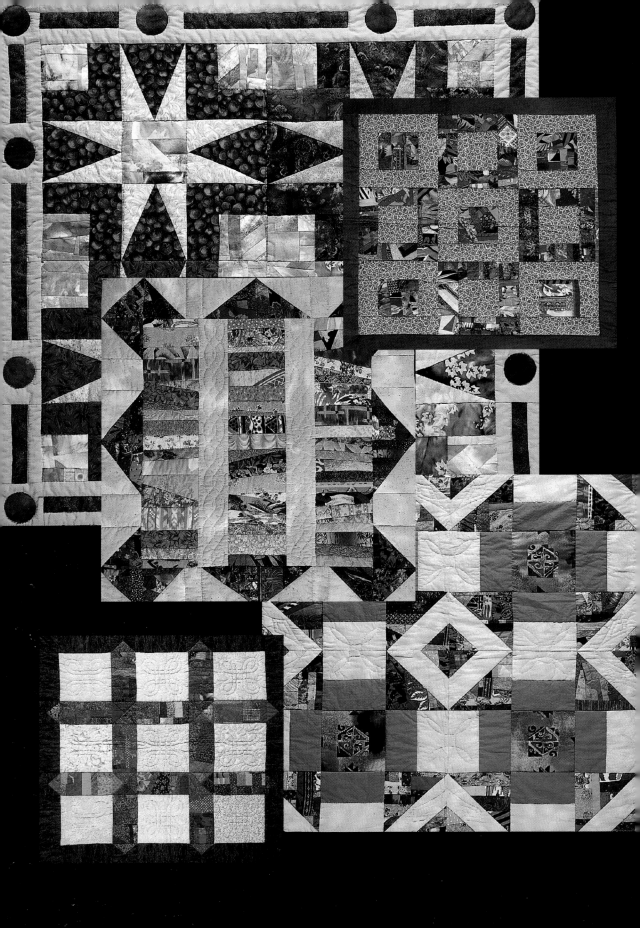

Chapter 4

Constructed Fabric Projects

The projects in this section, as well as those in the Gallery (Chapter 5), provide examples of many color schemes and showcase different types of constructed fabric. This variety illustrates the creative potential of constructed fabric when it's incorporated in quilts and wearable art. I hope these examples inspire you to make use of your scraps in your own constructed fabric projects.

Each project includes a description of the type of constructed fabric that was used in it. This will help you decide which type of fabric to sew, since you'll see how it works in a finished product. Refer to Chapter 1 for specific explanations of each type of constructed fabric.

Most of the wall quilts are made of four or nine blocks, which allows me to show you many ideas in this book. This also means you won't need large amounts of constructed fabric to complete a project. You can add to the size of any of the quilts by sewing more blocks, but don't make a wall quilt much bigger than 36″ square, or you won't be able to fit very many on a wall.

The larger the quilt, the more viewing distance you need to display it properly. This is no different than looking at a large work of art—you have to stand a distance from it to best understand the complete picture.

When you look at the pictures of the quilts and study the drawings, keep in mind that in most cases you can substitute non-constructed fabric for constructed fabric and vice versa. Of course, you can (and should) customize the color schemes to fit your decor. Be adventurous—allow your creative impulses to take over.

Blocks and Sections

If a pattern calls for you to sew two triangles together to make a 3″ square, trim the square to size before you sew it onto another section. When I sew any quilt project, I always double check the size of the pieces before I sew them onto something else. If you sew two pieces together that each have a ⅛″ error, you will end with a ¼″ error and nothing will appear straight or symmetrical.

When sewing two pieces of constructed fabric together, you may have to sew over several large groups of seams. Do this carefully so you don't break a needle or skip a stitch. You can sometimes trim some of the bulk of the seam away.

If a seam line is close to and running parallel to your stitching line, it can force the presser foot off to the side, making it difficult to maintain an accurate ¼″ seam. To correct this, trim and press the seam after sewing to get the unit back to the correct size.

If a pattern calls for four Template B and four Template Br (reversed), place the template right side up on the right side of the fabric and cut out four pieces. Then flip the template over so that its wrong side is facing up and cut out four more pieces. This gives you four pieces of Template B and four pieces of Template Br. You will encounter a reverse pattern piece in the instructions for Peacefuol Strips on page 66.

Backing

Backing requirements are not specified for each project. I shop the sale bins for backing fabrics in quantities of approximately one yard. All-over prints, multicolored prints, texture prints, but not stripes, are fabrics that work well for backing. My quilting stitch is not perfect, so I rarely use solid colors as a backing, because my stitches would be very visible.

Borders

To get the most accurate measurement for the border length, measure across the center of the quilt, not along the outside edges, which tend to stretch slightly. The directions have allowed extra length for the border pieces.

Mark the beginning and end points on your border strip fabric, but don't cut it to length yet. First lay a border piece across the top of the quilt and pin it in place. It should easily ease in place, but if it doesn't, move the pins and give yourself a little more fabric to work with.

If the border piece is more than ¼" short, you may have a problem, which you'll be able to find by laying the quilt top out on the floor and looking for a piecing error where a seam appears uneven. I have a floor made of square tiles so I lay my project out and check for even edges against the square tiles. It's important to find the piecing problem that causes the quilt to measure differently at the top, middle, and bottom. If you don't correct the problem, the quilt will hang with a noticeable bow. Don't try to compensate for the problem by sewing on borders that are an inch longer than the middle measurement or the quilt will appear lopsided and you will always be unhappy with it.

The border measurements listed in the project directions include extra fabric to allow for slight variations that naturally occur when sewing pieces together.

Binding

There are several types of binding you can use on a quilt—single thickness straight edge, bias edge, or double thickness of either straight edge or bias. Since these projects are wall quilts and will not get much wear and tear, I recommend a single thickness straight edge binding.

I cut the binding 1⅛" wide and then sew the lengths together at right angles to achieve a miter joint. If you wish to use a double thickness binding or a bias binding, you'll need more fabric than indicated in the instructions.

Seam Allowances

None of the templates have seam allowances indicated, so remember to add ¼" on all sides. If a piece can be easily rotary cut, the cutting measurements are given in parenthesis. All border and sashing measurements include seam allowances because it is assumed you will rotary cut them.

Line Drawings

You will find line drawings of each project in Appendix A beginning on page 92. Copy these diagrams and experiment by coloring them differently and placing constructed fabric in different positions. By experimenting with the designs, you'll find new and exciting ways to use constructed fabrics.

Inspiration

My hope is that the projects shown here reveal the creative potential of constructed fabric and inspire you to sew beautiful items using designs from the book and your imagination.

For further inspiration, observe pictures of antique quilts, most of which contain some examples of string quilts or crazy quilts. Study Amish and Mennonite-made quilts to see how they used the crazy quilt technique with mostly solid color fabrics. Books of contemporary art quilts are another source of inspiration. All of these resources provide ideas for color schemes and block designs that you can adapt to your constructed fabric quilts and wearable art.

Purple Pinwheel

Designed and sewn by Joyce Mori and hand-quilted by Delores Stemple of Aurora, West Virginia.

This lovely wall quilt has a French country-side look to it and would be the perfect complement to a young girl's canopy bed. The constructed fabric is a medium-value Crazy quilt type (Block #9, page 11). There are 40 constructed triangles in this quilt, but you can alternate constructed and non-constructed triangles. The constructed fabric is made from every color imaginable, with the wrong sides of darker prints used to add variety. The simple white-on-white background allows the constructed fabric pieces to stand out.

Name of Quilt: Purple Pinwheel
Finished Quilt Size: 36″ x 36″
Skill Level: Beginner
Line Drawing on page 93

Fabric Chart
- ⅔ yard medium-value constructed fabric (about seven 12″ x 12″ pieces)
- ⅔ yard purple print (includes enough to make a single straight edge binding)
- 1 yard white-on-white fabric

Cutting Chart
Template A (from page 101)
- 40 medium-value constructed fabric
- 16 purple print
- 56 white-on-white
Template B (from page 102)
- 4 white-on-white
Borders
- 4 strips of purple fabric 2½″ x 38½″ for borders

Making the Quilt

This quilt is made by sewing rectangles, made of triangles, together. Sew strips of these rectangles onto the side, top, and bottom of the pinwheel center. Refer to the diagram to see how the pieces go together.

1. Sew a constructed A to a white A to form a square. Sew two of these squares together to form a rectangle. Make 20 of these rectangles.

2. Sew a purple A to a white A to form a square. Sew two of these squares together to form a rectangle. Make eight of these rectangles.

3. To make the center pinwheel, make a Unit 1 (Fig. 4-1) by sewing a Template B to one of the rectangles from Step 2. Make four of these units and sew them together with the triangles positioned as shown in the diagram.

4. Sew four strips, each of which has two rectangles from Step 1, then a rectangle from Step 2, and finally, another rectangle from Step 1. Sew one of these to the top and another to the bottom of the center pinwheel.

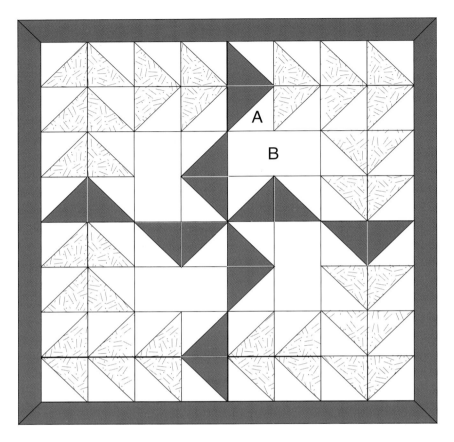

Purple Print

White

Constructed

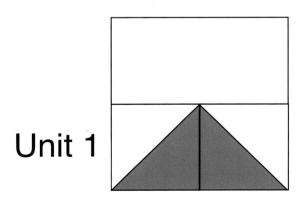

Unit 1

Figure 4-1

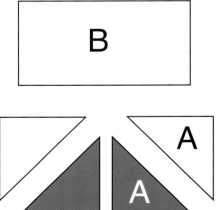

B

A

A

Figure 4-2

5. Sew the remaining rectangles together in sets of two. Sew one set to each end of the remaining strips from Step 4. Note the correct direction of the rectangle sets. Sew one strip to each side of the center pinwheel.

6. Double check the measurement for the outside purple borders. The borders on this quilt were mitered, but you may find it easier to use regular squared borders. Sew the top and bottom borders first. Trim the excess fabric even with the quilt top. Complete the quilt top by sewing on the side borders.

Quilting

1. Assemble the quilt top, batting, and backing together in a quilt sandwich and quilt as you wish. There's room in the white area of the center pinwheel to add a special quilting motif of your choice. The rest of the quilt is quilted in the ditch. The line of quilting ¾″ inside the pointed edge of the purple triangles holds the piecework to the backing and emphasizes the pinwheel.

2. Bind and label your quilt.

Slashing Squares

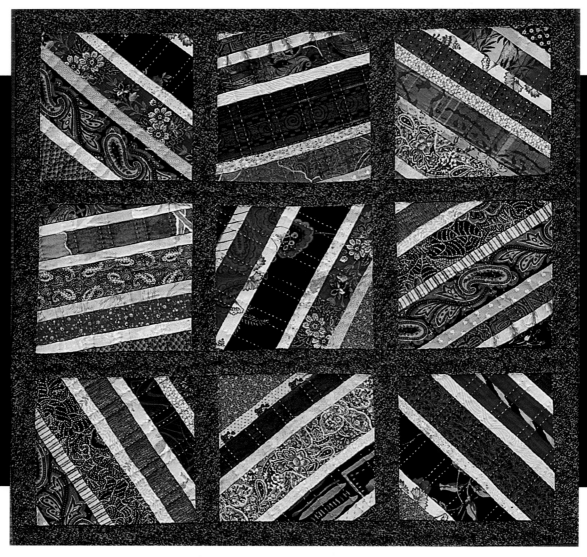

Designed, sewn, and hand-quilted by Joyce Mori.

This wall quilt is easy to do—cut out nine blocks from constructed fabric and sew them together with sashing strips. The Slashing blocks (Block #12, page 12) work very well with this simple arrangement because the light strips show direction and movement on the surface of the quilt. Most of the other types of constructed fabric would also work well. When using more complex types of constructed fabric, widen the sashing strips to accentuate the blocks.

Name of Quilt: Slashing Squares
Finished Quilt Size: 22″ x 22″
Skill Level: Beginner
Line Drawing on page 94

Fabric Chart
• 9 pieces of constructed fabric 8″ to 12″ square (this size allows you to place the template in different ways so the strips aren't always at a straight or horizontal angle)
Alternate: 22″ square piece regular fabric
• ½ yard navy print fabric for the sashing strips and single straight edge binding

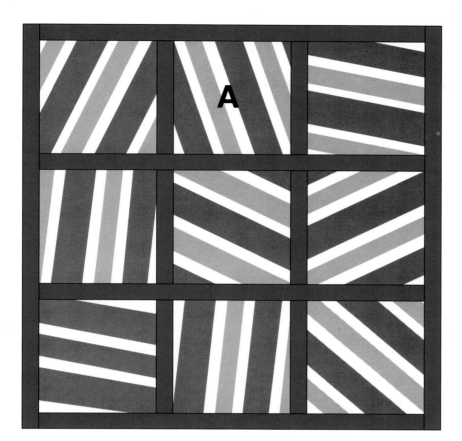

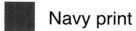 Navy print

Figure 4-3

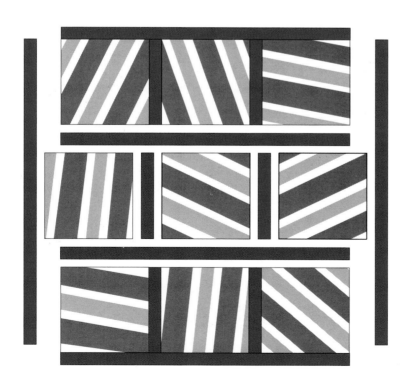

Figure 4-4

Cutting Chart

Template A (from page 104)
- 9 constructed fabric (vary the angle of the strips when you cut these out)

Borders
- 6 strips of navy fabric 1½″ x 6½″ for the sashing
- 4 strips of navy fabric 1½″ x 22½″ for the sashing and top borders (this allows some extra length)
- 2 strips of navy fabric 1½″ x 24½″ for the borders (this allows some extra length)

Notice the individual strips alternate a dark and a light. This reinforces the lines of the design.

Making the Quilt

For Slashing Squares simply sew nine constructed blocks together with sashing strips in between. Add the borders and your quilt top is ready for quilting and binding!

1. When cutting out the nine Template As from constructed fabric, turn the template in different ways so the direction of the strips varies. Refer to the diagram and sew three As together with a sashing strip between them. Make three rows of three squares each.

2. Connect the three rows by sewing a sashing strip between them. Trim the ends of all the sashing strips. You now have a nine-block unit sewn together.

3. Double check the measurement for the borders. Sew on the top and bottom borders first. Trim the fabric even with the quilt top. Complete the quilt top by sewing on the side borders.

Quilting

1. Assemble the quilt top, batting, and backing together in a quilt sandwich. I quilted in the ditch around each block, then in parallel lines across each block in the opposite direction of the actual slashing strips. Quilting lines are always difficult to see on printed fabrics, but if the slashing blocks are sewn of solid color fabrics, the quilting lines will be more visible.

2. Bind and label your quilt.

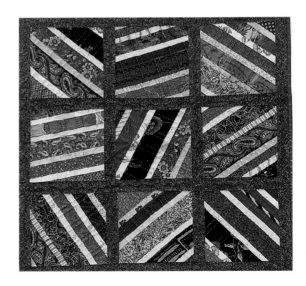

Turquoise Trail

Designed, sewn, and hand-quilted by Joyce Mori.

This quilt utilizes the traditional rail fence block. The major colors in the constructed fabric (Block #10, page 12) are turquoise, green, purple, orange, and rust. Two varieties of beige, one slightly lighter than the other, set off the bright Southwestern colors. You could easily make this a Christmas quilt by substituting red/green constructed fabric.

Name of Quilt: Turquoise Trail
Finished Size of Quilt: 36" x 36"
Skill Level: Beginner
Line Drawing on page 94

Turquoise Trail

Fabric Chart
• 9 12″ squares constructed fabric (Hint: scraps from cutting Template A can be joined to other scraps to make another piece of constructed fabric.) *Alternate: 36″ x 36″ piece regular fabric*
• ⅔ yard light beige print
• 1 yard darker beige print (includes enough to make a single straight edge binding)

Cutting Chart
Template A (from page 103)
• 36 constructed fabric
Template B (from page 105)
• 36 light beige print
• 36 darker beige print

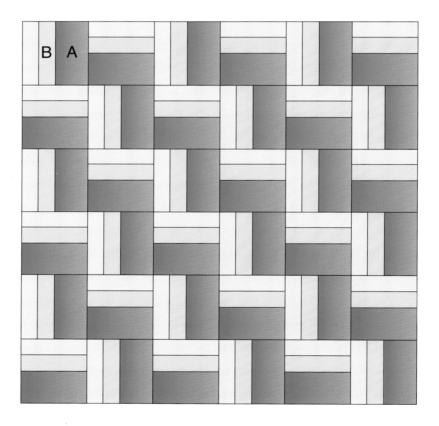

Figure 4-5

☐ Beige Print #1

☐ Beige Print #2

▨ Constructed Fabric

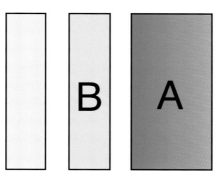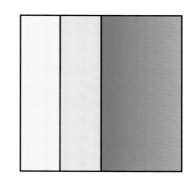

Figure 4-6

Making the Quilt

Turquoise Trail is made with 36 squares sewn in six rows. Make the squares by sewing a Template A to two Template Bs as shown in Figure 4-6. When you're ready to sew the rows, alternate the direction of the squares.

1. Sew a Template A to one dark beige B and one light beige B to form a square. Note that the darker beige is closest to the constructed fabric. Make 36 squares.

2. Study the diagram and sew six squares together to form a row. Make six rows.

Note that there are two types of rows—one begins with a vertical striped block and the other begins with a horizontal striped block.

3. Sew the rows together to complete the quilt top.

Quilting

1. Assemble the quilt top, batting, and backing together in a quilt sandwich. I quilted in the ditch around the templates then in a line down the center of each light beige piece to reinforce the path of the design across the quilt.

2. Bind and label your quilt.

Designed, sewn, and hand-quilted by Joyce Mori.

I call this an art quilt because it features constructed fabric sewn with bright solid colors combined with black and white prints and black solid (Block #16, page 14). The combination of colors reminds me of quilts by Yvonne Porcella, a contemporary quilt artist. This very modern quilt project is perfect for contemporary decor.

Name of Quilt: **An Art Quilt for Anyone**
Finished Size of Quilt: 26″ x 33″
Skill Level: Beginner
Line Drawing on page 95

Fabric Chart
• 4 16″ squares constructed fabric (use leftovers to create more constructed fabric and remember to add black and white fabrics with vivid stripes or checks with the bright solid colors)
• 1 yard solid black (includes enough to make a single straight edge binding)
• 30 scraps of bright solid colored fabric large enough for 2½″ x 3½″ rectangles (seams included)

Cutting Chart
Template A (from page 104)
• 8 constructed fabric
Template B (from page 114)
• 30 bright solid colors (as many different colors as possible)
Template C (from page 106)
• 2 black
Sashing and Borders
• 2 pieces black 1½″ x 12½″
• 8 pieces black 2½″ x 12½″
• 2 pieces black 2½″ x 27½″ for top and bottom borders

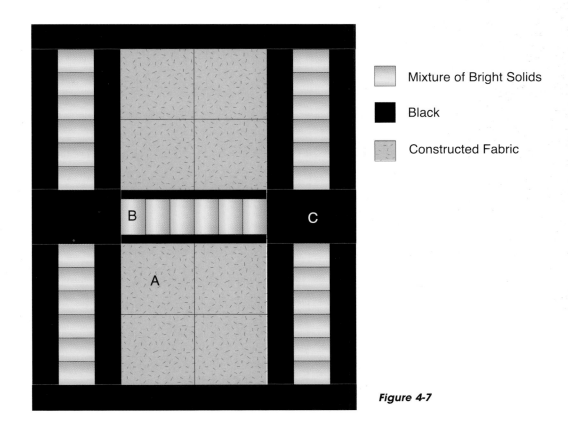

Mixture of Bright Solids

Black

Constructed Fabric

Figure 4-7

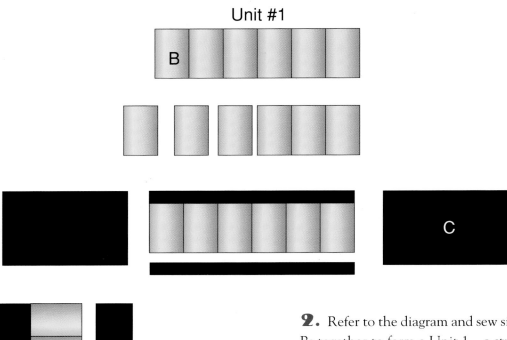

Unit #1

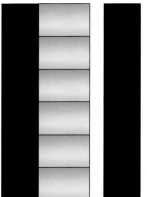

Figure 4-8

Making the Quilt

Four constructed fabric Template As form each of the two center blocks of this quilt. Using lots of different bold solid colors in the Template B strips adds vibrancy and the black connecting pieces set the colors off beautifully.

1. Sew four Template As together to form a block. Make two blocks.

2. Refer to the diagram and sew six Template Bs together to form a Unit 1—a strip of bright solid color rectangles (see Fig. 4-8). Make five Unit 1s.

3. Sew a 1½″ black sashing strip to each long side of a Unit 1, then sew a Template C to each end (see Fig. 4-8).

4. Sew a 2½″ black sashing strip to each long side of the four remaining Unit 1s. Refer to the diagram and sew one of these sets to the two opposite sides of a constructed block. Repeat this for the other constructed block.

5. Sew the three sections together.

6. Sew on the top and bottom borders.

Quilting

1. Assemble the quilt top, batting, and backing together in a quilt sandwich. I quilted in the ditch over much of the quilt and around many of the separate patches in each constructed block.

2. Bind and label your quilt.

Diagonals

Designed, sewn, and hand-quilted by Joyce Mori.

This quilt features the Diagonals constructed fabric type #11 on page 12. These very graphic blocks with strong directional lines are placed so the lines point in different directions. Because the blocks are set on point, the quilt has an interesting and lively appearance.

Many different types of constructed fabric blocks can be used in this wall quilt design which puts emphasis on each individual block. If you use a plain color fabric for the spacer blocks and the outside framing triangles, you can add detailed hand or machine quilting for more visual texture in the design.

I made the framing triangles extra large to give the appearance of blocks floating on the gray surface. Trimming the triangles even with the tips of the constructed blocks will slightly change the final size of the wall quilt.

Name of Quilt: Diagonals
Finished Size of Quilt: 25½" x 25½"
Skill Level: Beginner to Intermediate
Line Drawing on page 95

Fabric Chart

- 9 6″ squares constructed fabric (sew each square separately and then trim it to the correct size. *Alternate: 24″ x 24″ piece regular fabric.*
- fat quarter red print (18″ x 22″)
- ½ yard gray print (includes enough to make a single straight edge binding)

Cutting Chart

Template A (from page 104)
- 9 constructed fabric
- 4 red print

Misc.
- 2 11″ squares gray print
- 2 7½″ squares gray print

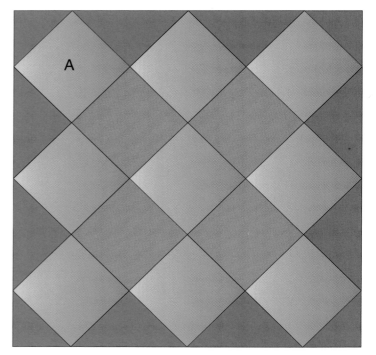

Figure 4-12

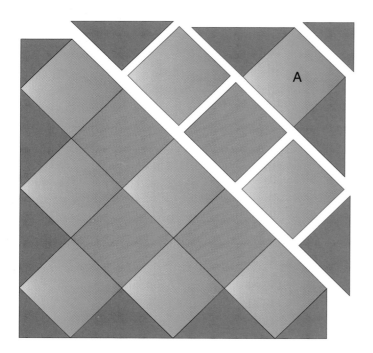

Figure 4-13

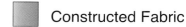 Constructed Fabric

 Gray

 Red

Making the Quilt

In Diagonals, the 13 squares are sewn together in diagonal rows with triangles on the outer edges.

1. Cut each of the 11″ squares in half and half again as shown in Figs. 4-9 and 4-10 for a total of eight triangles (the triangles for the four sides).

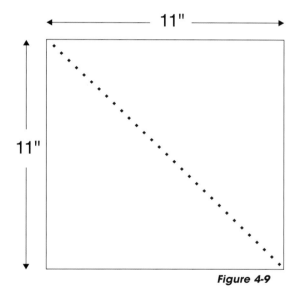

Figure 4-9

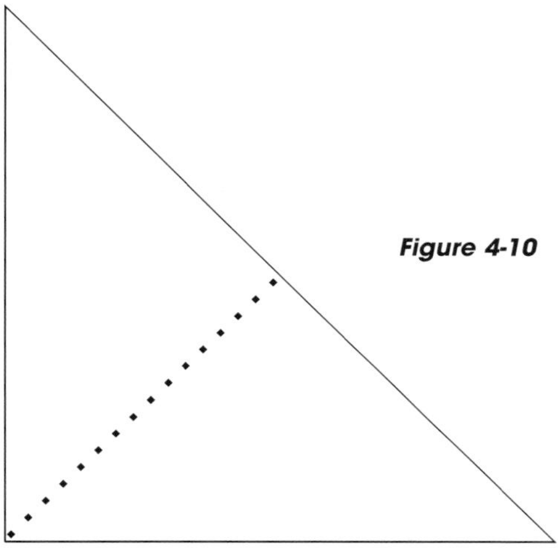

Figure 4-10

2. Cut each of the 7½″ squares in half as shown in Fig. 4-11 for a total of four small triangles (the corner triangles).

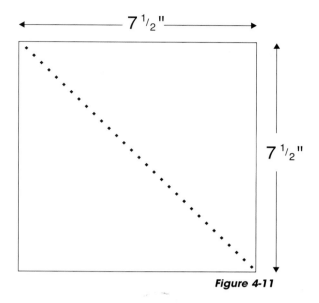

Figure 4-11

3. Refer to Fig. 4-13 and sew the diagonal rows as shown.

4. Sew the rows together to form the quilt top. Notice that the side triangles extend beyond the edges of the quilt This is what makes it look like there is an additional small border beyond the squares and the squares appear to float on the surface. You can trim off this excess if you wish.

Quilting

1. Assemble the quilt top, batting, and backing together in a quilt sandwich and quilt as you wish. I quilted a motif in each red square, in the ditch around the slashing blocks, around each strip, and in parallel lines in the gray framing triangles.

2. Bind and label your quilt.

Squares: Solid and Hollow

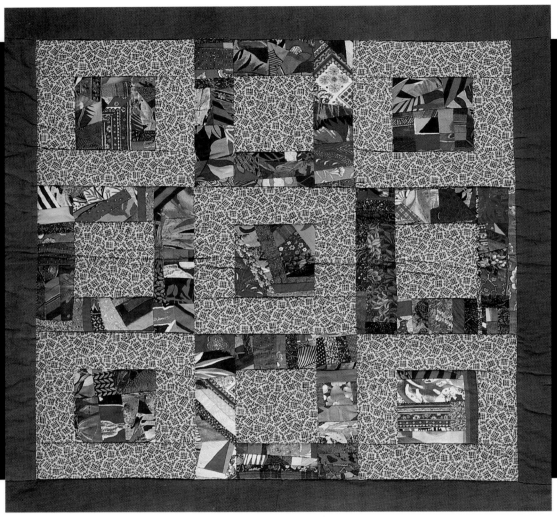

Designed and sewn by Joyce Mori and hand-quilted by Delores Stemple of Aurora, West Virginia.

This quilt features constructed fabric sewn from wild prints. The fabrics are mostly dark and dark/mediums, but there are a few random light pieces sewn in. There isn't much of a selection process involved in sewing this fabric type (Block #10, page 12). It's just a matter of sewing together lots of prints and a few solids. I used very few solids because I didn't have many among my scraps.

Before choosing the background fabric, sew the constructed fabric and decide what background will best complement it. The navy print shown here blends well with the many colors in the constructed fabric.

To make a baby quilt with this design, use soft pastel prints for the constructed fabric and appliqué a small motif (perhaps a flower or teddy bear) in the center squares of the commercial print (see the Gingham Dogs and Calico Cats on page 88). By incorporating scraps of clothing from the baby's relatives you can make this an especially meaningful heirloom quilt.

Name of Quilt: Squares: Solid and Hollow
Finished Size of Quilt: 35″ x 35″
Block Size: 10″
Skill Level: Beginner
Line Drawing on page 96

Fabric Chart
- 5 12″ squares constructed fabric. *Alternate: 27″ x 27″ piece regular fabric*
- ⅔ yard navy print
- ½ yard navy solid (includes enough for a single straight edge binding)

Cutting Chart
Template A (from page 107)
- 5 constructed fabric
- 4 navy print

Template B (from page 105)
- 8 constructed fabric
- 10 navy print
Template C (from page 108)
- 8 constructed fabric
- 10 navy print
Borders
- 2 strips navy solid 3″ x 33″ (extra allowed)
- 2 strips navy solid 3″ x 37″ (extra allowed)

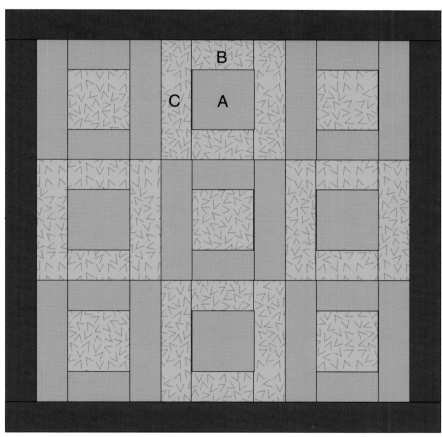

Figure 4-14

 Navy Print　　 Navy Solid

Constructed

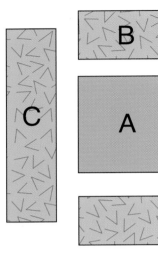
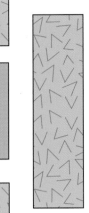

Figure 4-15

Making the Quilt

For this quilt, you make nine squares consisting of one Template A, two Template Bs, and two Template Cs. In five of the squares, a constructed center is framed by navy and in the other four squares, a navy center is framed by constructed fabric. Alternate these squares when sewing the rows as shown in Fig. 4-14.

1. Refer to Fig. 4-15 and sew a constructed Template B to the top and bottom of a navy Template A. Then sew a constructed Template C on each of the sides to form a complete square with a navy print center. Make four squares with navy print centers.

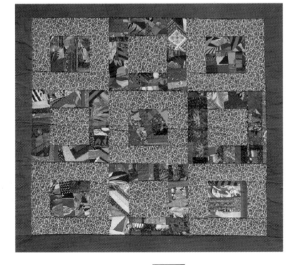

2. For the other five squares, sew a navy Template B to the top and bottom of a constructed Template A. Then sew a navy Template C on each of the sides to form a complete square with a constructed fabric center. Make five squares with constructed fabric centers.

3. Refer to Fig. 4-14 and sew the squares together to form three rows, then sew the rows together.

4. Sew on the two side borders first and finish by sewing on the top and bottom borders. Be sure to double check the measurements before cutting the borders.

Quilting

1. Assemble the quilt top, batting, and backing together in a quilt sandwich and quilt as you wish. If you use a solid color for the border, you can add some fancy quilting.

2. Bind and label your quilt.

Gradations

Designed and sewn by Joyce Mori and hand-quilted by Delores Stemple of Aurora, West Virginia.

Several years ago I purchased a set of samples of lovely dyed fabrics from True Colors in Pittstown, New Jersey. When I came across these pieces recently, I knew they were too lovely to throw away so I designed this quilt to showcase them. Though the solid color gradations are striking in this quilt, which uses a modified constructed fabric type #14 (page 13), this design would work with any collection of small samples of fabric you have. Many of you probably belong to a fabric club where you receive such samples on a regular basis.

Even though the drawing for this quilt shows the gradation rectangles all equal in size, in my quilt they are not. I wanted to use a more improvisational method, in keeping with the idea behind constructed fabric. In any case,

what you must achieve is a rectangle 1″ wide and 8″ long (finished size). The way you sew the scraps together and the number of scraps you use is your choice. The line drawing shows the general idea.

I selected six samples of fabric and sewed them together from light to dark. I then trimmed this rectangle to size, which resulted in the two end rectangles being a different size than the ones in the middle. I didn't want to stop and cut each fabric sample to the exact size needed for exact uniformity in the rectangles. The effect is the same—you see the shading from light to dark within the color group.

The corners on the borders each require seven rectangles which I trimmed to size after sewing them onto the black print section of the border. I ended up with different sizes in the corner, which is a reflection of the size of the sample fabrics I was working with and the final size of the quilt top. Remember that the gradation sections in this quilt are not intended to be composed of template cut pieces. You just sew and trim to size and what happens, happens. The final result will look lovely.

Name of Quilt: Gradations
Finished Size of Quilt: 26″ x 26″
Skill Level: Beginner to Intermediate
Line Drawing on page 96

Fabric Chart
- 17 1½″ wide strips gradated fabric in various lengths and colors (see cutting chart below).
Alternate: fat quarter regular fabric (18″ x 22″)
- ¾ yard black print (includes enough to make a single straight edge binding)
- ⅔ yard white-on-white print

Cutting Chart
Template A (from page 111)
- 18 white on white print
Template B (from page 111)
- 18 black print

Template C (from page 111)
- 18 white on white print
Misc.
- 9 strips gradated fabric 1½″ x 8½″ (includes seam allowances)
- 4 strips gradated fabric 1½″ x 5½″ (includes seam allowances)
- 4 strips gradated fabric 1½″ x 4½″ (includes seam allowances)
- 4 strips black print fabric 1½″ x 16½″

Figure 4-16

☐ White on White   ▨ Gradated Rectangle

■ Black

Figure 4-17

Making the Quilt

The nine squares in Gradations are made of six triangles (two Template As, two Bs, and two Cs) joined by a gradated strip of six colors. When you sew the squares into rows, alternate the direction of the strips for a dramatic effect.

1. Refer to Fig. 4-17 and sew a Template A to a Template B, then add a Template C to form a rectangle. Trim the rectangle to 3½″ x 8½″. Make 18 of these rectangles.

2. Join two of the rectangles with a 8½″ gradated strip to form a square. Make nine of these squares.

3. Refer to Fig. 4-17 and sew the squares together into three rows.

4. Sew the three rows together to form the unbordered quilt top.

5. Sew a 4½″ gradated strip to each end of a black strip to form the top border. Repeat for the bottom border and sew them to the quilt. Trim if necessary.

6. Sew a 5½″ gradated strip to each end of a black strip to form the right border. Repeat for the left border and sew them to the quilt. If your quilt measures more than 24½″ across the center, you'll have to make these border strips longer. Don't worry if your quilt measures less than 24½″, just trim the ends off after sewing on the borders.

Quilting

1. Assemble the quilt top, batting, and backing together in a quilt sandwich and quilt as you wish. This quilt was outline quilted.

2. Bind and label your quilt.

A Taste of Amish

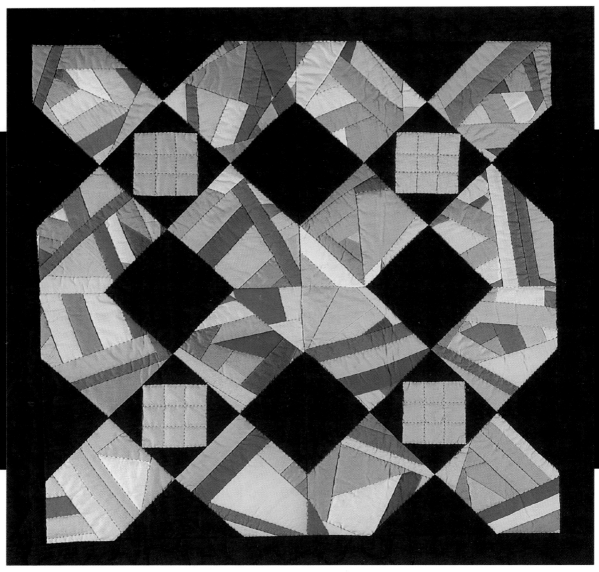

Designed, sewn, and hand-quilted by Joyce Mori.

This Amish-look project combines constructed fabric made of brightly colored solids (Block #5, page 11) with a black background.

Compare this quilt with A Taste of Amish, Triangles on page 90. Note that even though the colors are similar, A Taste of Amish, Triangles uses an equilateral triangle as the main pattern piece. The constructed fabric is repeated in one of the borders, which is an excellent way to use constructed fabric. Then compare this to Big X on page 88, which uses the same block as A Taste of Amish but has constructed fabric sewn from multicolored scraps for the main portion of the quilt. A few areas of light constructed fabric are used in the center square area.

When you analyze these three quilts, you can easily see how the type of constructed fabric used in a quilt changes the overall appearance.

Name of Quilt: A Taste of Amish
Finished Size of Quilt: 28″ x 28″
Skill Level: Intermediate
Line Drawing on page 97

Fabric Chart
• 2 20″ x 16″ pieces of constructed fabric
• ⅔ yard black solid (includes enough for a single straight edge binding)
• Scraps of 4 different solid colors

Cutting Chart
Template A (from page 122)
• 1 each of the 4 solid colors
Template B (from page 110)

• 16 constructed fabric
Template C (from page 109)
• 16 black
Template D (from page 109)
• 16 black
Borders
• 2 strips black 2½″ x 28½″ for the top and bottom borders (extra allowed)
• 2 strips black 2½″ x 30 ½″ for the side borders (extra allowed)

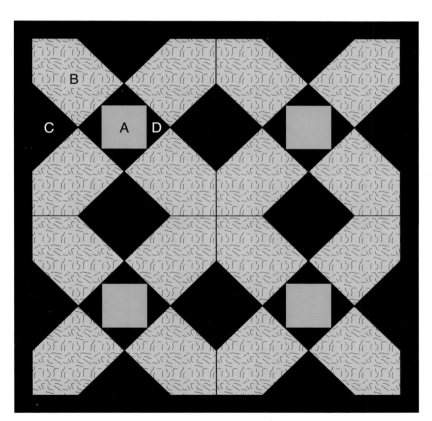

Figure 4-18

■ Black Background

▨ Constructed Fabric

▨ Solid Color

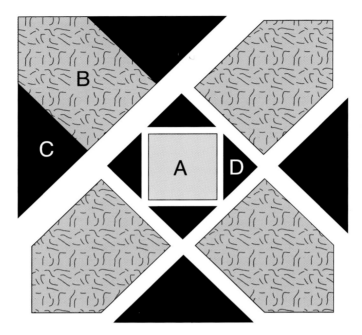

Figure 4-19

Making the Quilt

The four blocks in this quilt are made with one Template A surrounded by four Ds. Then four Bs and four Cs are added on to form a large square block, which is a quarter of the quilt.

1. Sew a Template D on each side of an A to form a square. Make four of these squares. Then sew a B on two opposite sides of the square as shown in Fig. 4-19. Repeat on each of the squares.

2. Sew a C on each long side of a B as shown in Fig. 4-19. Make eight of these units.

3. Refer to the diagram and sew two of these units to each of the units completed in Step 1 to complete one block, a quarter of the quilt. Make four blocks (each block is one quarter of the quilt).

4. Sew the blocks together to com-plete the quilt top.

5. Sew on the top and bottom borders and then the side borders.

Quilting

1. Assemble the quilt top, batting, and backing together in a quilt sandwich and quilt as you wish. I outline quilted many of the separate pieces in the constructed fabric. I used meander quilting on the borders and in several other areas of the black solid fabric.

2. Bind and label your quilt.

Serenity

Designed and sewn by Joyce Mori and hand-quilted by Delores Stemple of Aurora, West Virginia.

Three analogous color families—green, blue, and purple—of constructed fabric are used in this quilt, which uses fabric type #7 shown on page 11. In combination, these harmonious colors produce a quilt that is aptly named Serenity.

You don't need large amounts of constructed fabric to complete this quilt. I used constructed fabric for just the larger pieces but if you want to sew large amounts of constructed fabric, you can use it for the smaller squares too. Or you can use constructed fabric in the small squares and regular fabric for the large pieces.

The diagram is shaded to reflect only the color families—you decide where to use constructed fabric. Any three analogous (colors next to one another on the color wheel) will work for the color scheme of this quilt. Look at your scrap supply and choose colors that work best for you.

Name of Quilt: Serenity
Finished Size of Quilt: 40″ x 40″
Skill Level: Beginner
Line Drawing on page 97

Fabric Chart
- 15" x 20" piece purple constructed fabric
- 15" x 20" piece blue constructed fabric
- 15" x 20" piece green constructed fabric
- 12" square blue print
- 12" square green print
- ¾ yard beige print #1 (center beige)
- ¾ yard beige print #2 (includes enough for a straight edge binding)

Cutting Chart
Template A (from page 112)
- 8 purple constructed fabric
- 8 green constructed fabric
- 8 blue constructed fabric

- 16 beige print #1
- 8 beige print #2

Template B (from page 118)
- 16 blue print
- 16 green print
- 4 purple constructed fabric
- 16 beige print #1
- 20 beige print #2

Template C (from page 107)
- 2 blue constructed fabric
- 2 green constructed fabric
- 8 beige print #2

Template D (from page 105)
- 12 beige print #1
- 8 beige print #2

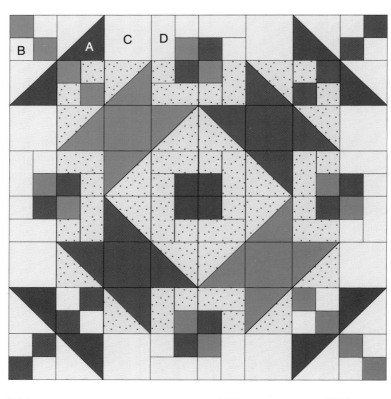

Figure 4-20

Beige Background - 1

Beige Background - 2

Green

Blue

Purple

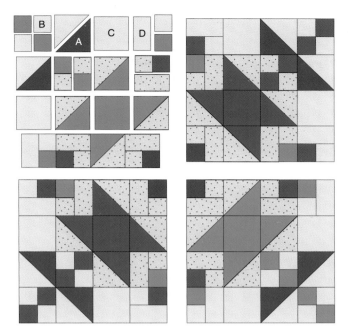

Figure 4-21

Making the Quilt

Even though there are lots of pieces in this quilt, they go together in logical steps. Take a few minutes to study Fig. 4-21 and sew the small units that make up the rows. Then sew four rows together to make a quarter, sew the quarters together, and it's ready for quilting and binding.

1. Refer to Fig. 4-21 and sew two Template As together to form a square. Make 24 squares, noting where to switch beige print #1 to #2, and where to use blue, purple, or green.

2. Again, refer to Fig. 4-21 and sew four Template B squares together to form a square patch unit. Make eight of these units.

3. Sew two Template B pieces together to form a rectangle and sew a Template D to this to make a square. Make 20 B-B-D squares.

When you look at the photo of the finished quilt, you can see that I tried this several different ways to find the best way. Fig. 4-21 shows the sewing method I preferred. However, there are several ways to sew the two Template B pieces to the rectangle and you can use any of them and still achieve the desired result.

4. Refer to Fig. 4-21 and sew the units together into four rows.

5. Sew four rows together to form a quarter section of the quilt. Repeat for the other three quarter sections, then sew the quarter sections together to form the quilt top.

Quilting

1. Assemble the quilt top, batting, and backing together in a quilt sandwich and quilt as you wish. This quilt was outline quilted with separate motifs placed around the center purple area.

2. Bind and label your quilt.

Peaceful Strips

Designed and sewn by Joyce Mori and hand-quilted by Delores Stemple of Aurora, West Virginia.

Here's a project to use up all those leftover strips of fabric that quilters always seem to end up with. Collect even and uneven-width strips that are at least 6″ wide and sew them together into fabric like Block #4 as shown on page 11. After you have sewn about eight strips together, you can trim the piece to a workable size. Cut the section so it is 6″ wide across the strips.

The predominate color value in this quilt is medium, but all colors and prints are combined to create a very attractive overall appearance.

Name of Quilt: Peaceful Strips
Finished Size of Quilt: 28″ x 32″
Skill Level: Intermediate
Line Drawing on page 98

Fabric Chart

• 3 12″ x 12″ squares dark-value constructed fabric. *Alternate for the dark-value constructed fabric: fat quarter (18″ x 22″) regular fabric*
• 3 5½″ x 24½″ strips medium-value constructed fabric
• ⅔ yard light fabric
• ¼ yard dark fabric for a single straight edge binding

Cutting Chart

Template A (from page 101)
• 12 dark constructed
• 12 light fabric

Template B (from page 119)
• 4 dark constructed
• 4 light fabric
Template Br (same as B, except reversed)
• 4 dark constructed
• 4 light fabric
Template C (from page 120)
• 4 light fabric
Template D (from page 118)
• 4 light fabric
Misc.
• 2 strips light fabric 3″ x 24½″ for center sashing (seams included)

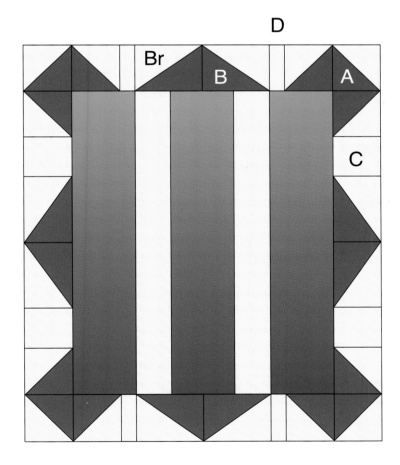

D Br B A C

Figure 4-22

☐ Light Fabric

▨ Constructed Fabric   ▨ Dark Constructed Fabric

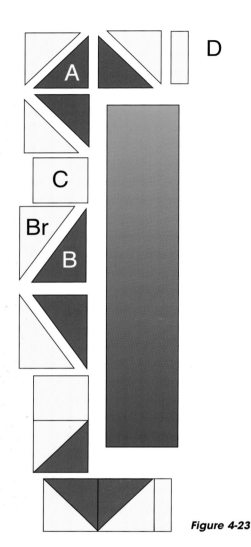

D

A

C

Br

B

Figure 4-23

Making the Quilt

The focal point of this quilt is the center made from three strips of constructed fabric, joined by sashing strips. Framing the center are four borders made by combining small pieces as shown in Fig. 4-23.

1. Sew the three strips of constructed fabric and trim them to the correct size of 5½" x 24½". I find it easier to sew small sections and then join them together rath er than create one 24½" unit all at once.

2. Sew the two sashing strips between the constructed fabric strips to create the main section of the quilt top.

3. Sew a dark Template A to a light A to form a square. Make 12 of these squares.

4. Sew a dark Template B to a light B to form a rectangle. Make four of these rectangles.

5. Sew a dark Template Br to a light Br to form a rectangle. Make four of these rectangles.

6. Refer to Fig. 4-23 and sew the four border strips, connecting the pieces with either a C or D as shown.

7. Sew the correct border strips on the top and bottom.

8. Sew a square from Step 3 on each end of the two remaining border strips and sew them on the sides.

Quilting

1. Assemble the quilt top, batting, and backing together in the quilt sandwich. I quilted a scroll motif in the center light panels and then quilted in the ditch for each strip of constructed fabric. I finished by quilting in the ditch for the rest of the quilt pieces.

2. Bind and label your quilt.

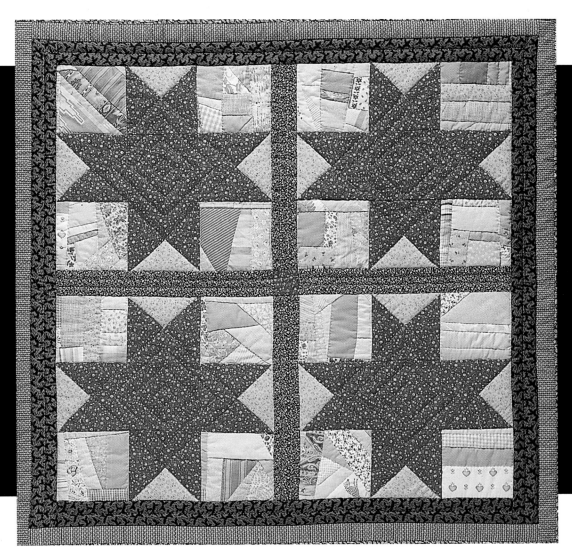

Designed, sewn, and hand-quilted by Joyce Mori.

This and the following project are star quilts—a popular design that's fun to sew and versatile enough to use for trying out different design ideas. The Star Block on page 23 and the Painted Stars on page 90 are also star quilts.

This quilt is called Country Charm because the red stars are sewn of calico and many of the prints in the constructed fabric (Block #10,

page 12) are very traditional. This design would be wonderful in a house decorated with an Early American or Country theme.

Name of Quilt: Country Charm
Finished Size of Quilt: 30½″ x 30½″
Skill Level: Beginner
Line Drawing on page 98

Country Charm

Fabric Chart
- 4 10″ x 10″ squares medium-value constructed fabric
- fat quarter medium blue print (18″ x 22″)
- fat quarter dark blue print (18″ x 22″)
- ½ yard red print #1
- ¼ yard red print #2 (for outer borders)
- ⅓ yard navy print (includes enough for a single straight edge binding)

Cutting Chart
Template A (from page 117)
- 16 medium blue print
- 16 red print #1
Template B (from page 103)
- 16 medium-value constructed
- 4 red print #1

Template C (from page 101)
- 16 red print #1
Template D (from page 117)
- 1 red print #1
Sashing and Borders (extra length is allowed for the borders)
- 4 2″ x 12½″ strips dark blue print (seams included) for sashing strips
- 2 2″ x 27″ strips navy print for top and bottom inner borders
- 2 2″ x 32″ strips navy print for side inner borders
- 2 1½″ x 30″ strips red print #2 for top and bottom outer borders
- 2 1½″ x 33″ strips red print #2 for side outer borders

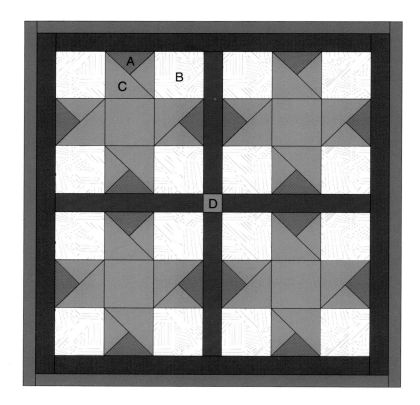

Figure 4-24

▨ Medium Blue Print	▦ Constructed	■ Dark Blue Print
■ Navy Print	▨ Red Print #1	▨ Red Print #2

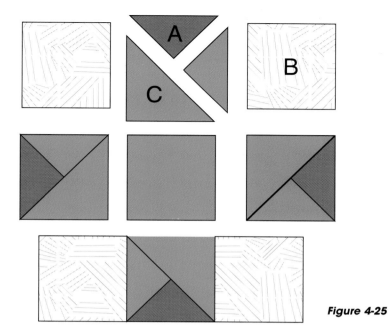

Figure 4-25

Making the Quilt

In Country Charm, the four star blocks are joined by sashing strips with a small square in the very center, then the center section is double bordered.

1. Refer to Fig. 4-25 and sew two As and a C to form a square, noting the placement of the red and blue pieces. Make 16 of these squares.

2. Sew one of these squares on opposite sides of a red Template B to form a row. Make four rows.

3. Sew a constructed Template B on opposite sides of one of the A-A-C squares from Step 1 to form a row. Make eight of these rows.

4. Refer to Fig. 4-25 and sew the three rows together to form a block. Make four blocks.

5. Join two of the blocks with a dark blue sashing strip to create a row. Make two rows.

6. Sew the small red square between two dark blue sashing strips to form the long center sashing strip. Connect the two rows with this strip.

7. Sew the shorter navy print inner border pieces to the top and bottom, trim, then sew on the longer navy print side border pieces. Trim.

8. Sew the shorter red print #2 outer border pieces to the top and bottom, trim, then sew on the longer red print #2 outer side border pieces. Trim.

Quilting

1. Assemble the quilt top, batting, and backing together in the quilt sandwich and quilt as you wish. I quilted in the ditch for the separate pieces in the constructed fabric blocks and in the ditch around all the pieces. I also quilted a series of squares on point inside the center of each red square.

2. Bind and label your quilt.

Bright Stars

Designed and sewn by Joyce Mori and hand-quilted by Delores Stemple of Aurora, West Virginia.

The stars in this quilt are vibrant and carefully set off by the light background and black border. Constructed fabric type #7 (page 11) is found in two places in this project—the square center of each star, and the black border. Type #9 (page 11) is found in the four light-colored squares in the center of the quilt.

This quilt is a popular choice for my constructed fabric workshops because it is easy to sew, uses small amounts of constructed fabric, and can be done in just about any set of colors.

Name of Quilt: Bright Stars
Finished Quilt Size: 26" x 26"
Skill Level: Beginner
Line Drawing on page 99

Fabric Chart

- 4 9″ squares of different single-color dark-value constructed fabrics
- 2 14″ squares black constructed fabric for the borders. (I sew a square and cut it into 2½″ sections and sew them together to achieve the required length.) *Alternate: 12″ x 27″ piece regular fabric*
- 12″ square light constructed fabric
- 4 12″ squares light fabric (each star uses a different light fabric)
- 4 12″ squares dark fabric (each star uses a different dark fabric)
- ¼ yard for single straight edge binding

Cutting Chart

Template A (from page 104)

- 1 of each green, purple, blue, and red constructed

Template B (from page 114)

- 8 green
- 8 purple
- 8 blue
- 8 red
- 32 light fabric

Template C (from page 122)

- 12 light fabric
- 4 light constructed fabric

Borders (includes seam allowance)

- 2 2½″ x 26″ strips black constructed fabric for the top and bottom
- 2 2½″ x 28″ strips black constructed fabric for the sides

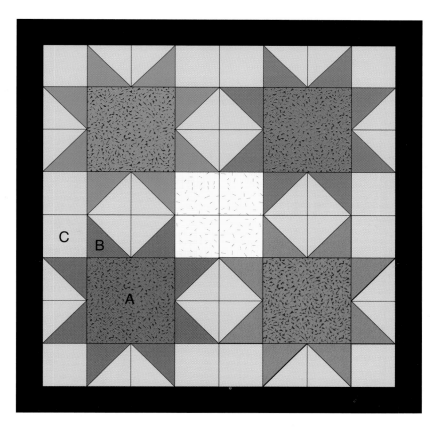

Figure 4-26

Blue Constructed	Blue Print	Black Constructed	Light Constructed
Green Constructed	Green Print	Red Constructed	Red Print
Various Light Fabrics		Purple Constructed	Purple Print

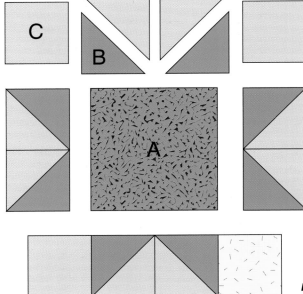

Figure 4-27

Making the Quilt

The four stars in this quilt are made with constructed centers and coordinating non-constructed points. The four light constructed squares in the center of the quilt and the black constructed borders really show off the range of possibilities when using constructed fabric.

1. For each of the star blocks, sew eight squares comprised of one light B and one dark B. Refer to Fig. 4-26 to see how the different fabric Template Bs are sewn into squares.

2. Sew two of these squares together to form the star points. Make four sets of star points for each star block. Sew one set of star points to each side of Template A.

3. Refer to Fig. 4-27 and sew a Template C on two sets of star points to form a strip.

4. Sew one of these strips on the top and the bottom of the previous unit to form a star block (i.e. purple star points on the purple constructed Template A, etc.).

5. Sew the four star blocks together.

6. Double check the measurement for the outside borders. If necessary, trim the fabric and sew on the top and bottom borders first, then complete the quilt top by sewing on the side borders.

Quilting

1. Assemble the quilt top, batting, and backing together in a quilt sandwich and quilt as you wish. This is quilted in the ditch and on the separate patches of the star centers in the ditch.

2. Bind and label your quilt.

Colorful Sashing

Designed and sewn by Joyce Mori and hand-quilted by Delores Stemple of Aurora, West Virginia.

This quilt uses constructed fabric type #7 sewn into sections of very specific colors—in this case, purple, orange, green, blue, and red. If you use some or all solid color fabrics in each unit, you will reinforce the specific color of that section. You can vary the placement of the colors and the number of colors you use. Your scrap supply will dictate how many pieces of each color you use. I used three blues and three purples and only two of the other colors because I had more blue and purple scraps.

The light center squares are a range of different prints (some are the wrong side of a darker

fabric). The triangles at the end of each sashing rectangle are cut from a single piece of fabric rather than constructed fabric because it can be difficult to sew four constructed triangles of this size where the sashings meet. The single triangle also helps reinforce the specific color of the section.

Name of Quilt: Colorful Sashing
Finished Size of Quilt: 40″ x 40″
Skill Level: Beginner
Line Drawing on page 99

Colorful Sashing

Fabric Chart
- 12 7" x 10" strips of differently colored constructed fabric
- 9 10" squares of different light fabrics.
Alternate: ¾ yard of one light fabric
- ¾ yard black (includes enough for a single straight edge binding)
- scraps of fabric colors to match sashing

Cutting Chart
Template A (from page 113)
- 12 constructed fabric (I used 2 orange, 2 green, 2 red, 3 blue, 3 purple)
- 8 black print

Template B (from page 117)
- 24 of colors to match your constructed fabric (I used 4 orange, 4 green, 4 red, 6 purple, 6 blue)
- 24 black print

Template C (from page 115)
- 9 of various light prints

Sashing and Borders
- 4 4½" x 12½" strips black print for longer border plus corner sashing units

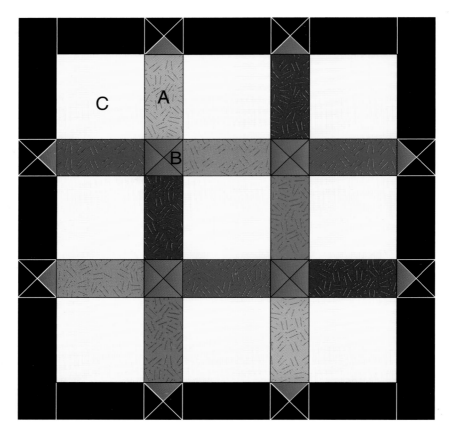

Figure 4-28

☐ Light Prints	▨ Constructed Fabric *(blue, red, green, and purple)*
■ Black	▨ Print to Match Sashing

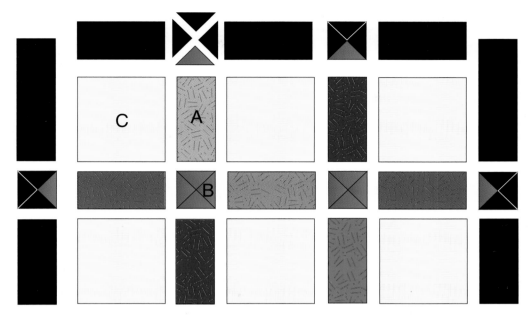

Figure 4-29

Making the Quilt

Before sewing any pieces together, lay them all out on the floor or pin them to a design wall to determine the best color placement. Use the photo and Fig. 4-28 to guide you.

1. Sew three Template Cs into a row with a constructed A between them. Make three of these rows.

2. Refer to Fig. 4-29 to sew four Bs into a small square. Sew four of these small squares, which will be used in the sashing strips.

3. Sew one colored B to three black Bs to form a small square. Sew eight of these small squares, which will be used in the borders.

4. For the connecting strips, sew three As and two of the B squares into a strip as shown. Make two connecting strips and sew them between the three rows to complete the main quilt body.

5. Use two of the squares from Step 3 to connect three black As in a border strip. Make two strips which, are the top and bottom borders, and sew them on.

6. Use two of the squares from Step 3 to connect two 12½" black strips and a black A in a border strip. Make two strips, which are the side borders, and sew them on.

Quilting

1. Assemble the quilt top, batting, and backing together in a quilt sandwich. This quilt features a single motif quilted in the light square areas and the rest is quilted in the ditch around the major pieces.

2. Bind and label your quilt.

Southwestern Themes

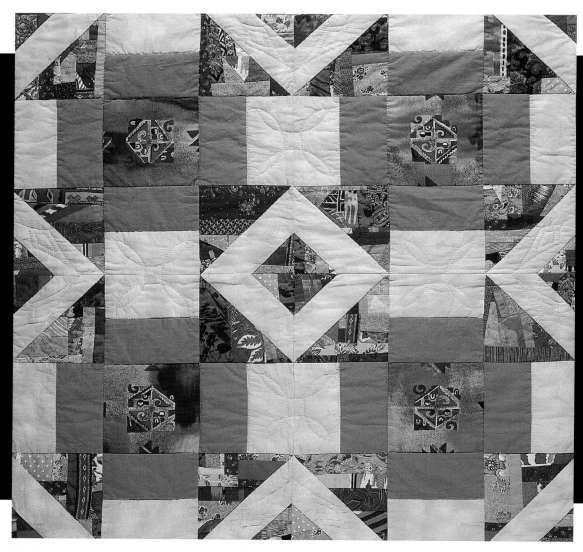

Designed and sewn by Joyce Mori and hand-quilted by Delores Stemple of Aurora, West Virginia.

The constructed fabric (Block #10, page 12) in this quilt features orange, brown, and rust with a beige background to set off the blocks. The touch of turquoise adds a sparkle of brightness to the overall design and the center of each quarter block showcases a preprinted Indian motif.

You can select any type of preprinted motif for the center of the block and choose your other colors to match. There are so many wonderful motifs available—animals, fishing, golf, flowers, etc.—you can customize this quilt to suit any taste.

Name of Quilt: Southwestern Themes
Finished Size of Quilt: 36″ x 36″
Skill Level: Beginner
Line Drawing on page 100

Fabric Chart
• 3 14″ squares constructed fabric. *Alternate: ½ yard regular fabric*
• ⅓ yard turquoise fabric
• ⅔ yard beige background fabric
• 4 preprinted motifs, each 6½″ square, seams included (The exact amount of fabric you need depends on the repeat pattern of the motif on the fabric.)
• ¼ yard rust fabric for a single straight edge binding

Cutting Chart
Template A (from page 114)
• 16 constructed fabric
Template B (from page 116)
• 16 beige
Template C (from page 121)
• 16 constructed fabric
Template D (from page 103)
• 16 turquoise
• 16 beige
Template E (from page 103)
• 4 preprinted panel fabric

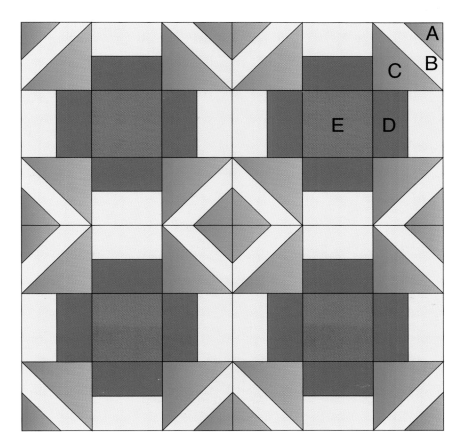

Figure 4-30

Beige   Turquoise

Constructed Fabric   Motif Fabric

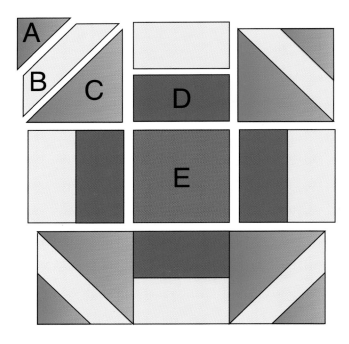

Figure 4-31

Making the Quilt

This quilt is made by making four identical blocks and joining them together.

1. Sew a turquoise Template D to a beige D to form a square. Make 16 of these squares.

2. Sew a constructed Template A to a beige B, then add a constructed C to form a square as shown in Fig. 4-31. Make 16 of these squares.

3. Sew one of these squares to each side of a D-D square as shown to make a row. Make eight of these rows.

4. Sew one of the remaining D-D squares to each side of a preprinted panel to make a row. Make four of these rows.

5. Refer to Fig. 4-30 and connect three rows to form one block, a quarter of the quilt top.

6. Join the four blocks together as shown to form the complete quilt top.

Quilting

1. Assemble the quilt top, batting, and backing together in a quilt sandwich. This quilt features some special motifs quilted in some of the larger beige areas. There's also quilting in the ditch around the separate pieces.

2. Bind and label your quilt.

Shades of Red

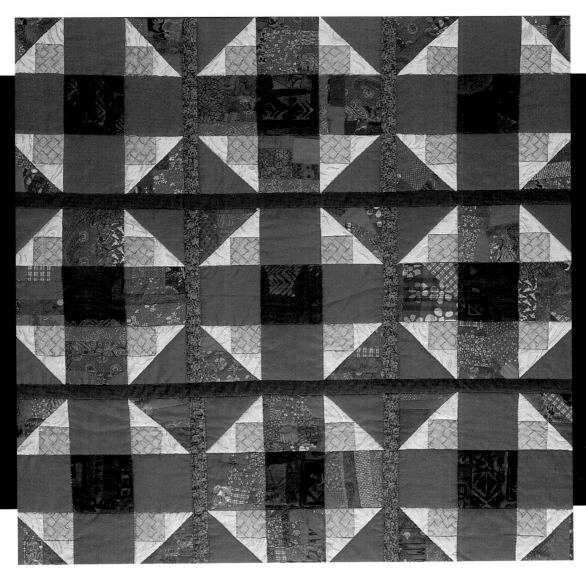

Designed, sewn, and hand-quilted by Joyce Mori.

This quilt proves the theory that all reds blend with one another. The constructed fabric (Block #7, page 11) consists of all types of fabrics, solids and prints, in a wide variety of reds—burgundy, bright red, fuchsia, orange red, etc. I think the combinations turned out quite lively. I used small amounts of green and navy in the quilt which is a perfect color scheme for a Christmas quilt.

Be adventurous and try different color combinations. One of the wonderful things about constructed fabric is that you can combine a wide variety of colors and yet the final result is always interesting and useful.

Name of Quilt: Shades of Red
Finished Size of Quilt: 38" x 38"
Skill Level: Intermediate
Line Drawing on page 100

Shades of Red

Fabric Chart
- 7 12″ x 10″ pieces red constructed fabric.
Alternate: ⅔ yard regular fabric
- ⅔ yard red print
- fat quarter medium pink (18″ x 22″)
- fat quarter green/blue print (18″ x 22″)
- fat quarter dark green print (18″ x 22″)
- ½ yard pale pink
- ¼ yard navy (includes enough for a single straight edge binding)

Cutting Chart
Template A (from page 103)
- 16 red constructed
- 20 red print
- 9 blue/green print
Template B (from page 101)
- 20 red constructed
- 16 red print
Template C (from page 121)
- 72 pale pink
Template D (from page 122)
- 36 medium pink
Misc.
- 6 pieces green print 1½″ x 13½″ for vertical sashing
- 2 strips navy fabric 1½″ x 40½″ for horizontal binding

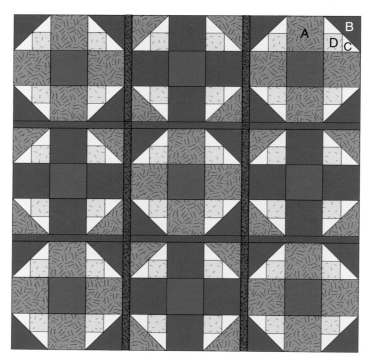

Figure 4-32

Red Constructed	Dark Green Print
Red Print	Navy
Pink Print	Light Print
Blue/Green Print	

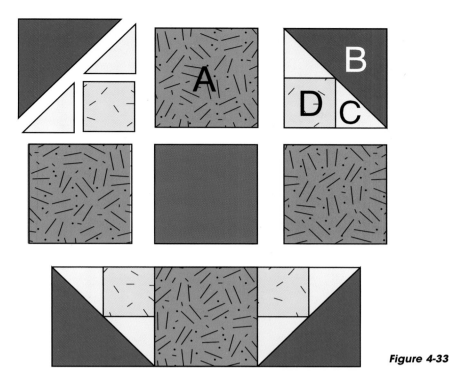

Figure 4-33

Making the Quilt

The nine blocks in this quilt are joined with green print and navy sashing strips. Each block has a dark green center.

1. Refer to Fig. 4-33 and sew two Template Cs to a D to form a triangle. Make 36 of these triangles.

2. Sew one of these triangles to a red constructed B to form a square. Make 20 of these squares.

3. Sew one of these squares on either side of a red print A to form a row. Make 10 rows.

4. Sew a red print A on opposite sides of a blue/green A to form a row. Make five rows.

5. Refer to Fig. 4-32 and sew three rows together to form a block. Make five blocks.

6. Sew a red print B to a triangle from Step 1 to form a square. Make 16 squares.

7. Sew one of these squares on opposite sides of a red constructed A to form a row. Make eight rows.

8. Sew a red constructed A on either side of a blue/green A to form a row. Make four rows.

9. Refer to Fig. 4-32 and sew three rows together to form a block. Make four blocks.

10. Sew the green print sashing strips between the blocks as indicated on Fig. 4-32.

11. Sew the navy sashing strips between the rows of blocks to complete the quilt top.

Quilting

1. Assemble the quilt top, batting, and backing together in a quilt sandwich and quilt as you wish. This quilt is quilted in the ditch.

2. Bind and label your quilt.

Chapter 5

The Gallery

Wearable Art

My favorite piece of clothing for wearable pieces is the vest. A vest can set off a skirt and blouse combination or dress up a top and pair of pants. In the spring and fall, a vest provides just enough warmth to take off an early morning or late night chill. Vests are simple to cut out and sew and are easy to adapt to a variety of decorating techniques.

The photo gallery features several vests made with constructed fabric. Select a vest pattern from my list of favorites (Appendix C, page 123) or find a favorite of your own.

Depending on the style of the vest and the type of fabric you use, you may want to use a foundation fabric to add stability, shaping, and a layer of warmth. I generally use muslin for the foundation fabric and don't sew each scrap to it, but instead sew on units of the vest. For example, I would sew rows of constructed fabric and then sew each row separately onto the foundation. I start at the side or top of the vest piece and sew on units until I reach the other side or bottom.

Under the descriptions of each vest I note if it's made with a foundation fabric. You can omit the foundation fabric if you want to sew the vest sections following the pattern directions, but you will need to use iron-on interfacing on each vest front piece to give it some shaping and stability.

Select a vest pattern with fairly straight lines, without body shaping elements such as darts or fitted princess styles. Constructed fabric works much better in such patterns and the straight lines of the garment allow the constructed fabric to be the focus of the design.

Formality

Designed and sewn by Joyce Mori.

This vest is made with a light-value constructed fabric in the crazy quilt style. As you can see, the constructed fabric (made from cotton fabrics) is used on the lower third of the vest fronts and back.

The lovely floral fabric is a remnant of drapery fabric that adds formality to the vest design. The lining is plain white drapery lining. Both fabrics are machine washable and I washed them before sewing to allow for shrinkage and to make sure they would hold up to machine washing. (I wear my vests a lot and want them to be machine washable.)

Because the drapery fabric and lining are heavier than normal quilter's cottons, there's no need for a foundation fabric. I didn't quilt the vest, which is from a simple no-seam bolero pattern.

Samples

Designed and sewn by Joyce Mori. The pattern is the Cat-Crazy Vest from O'Dell House.

I wanted to make a jacket from Guatemalan ikat fabric so I sent to a number of mail order sources to get samples of their fabrics. The samples were too pretty to throw away so I used them to construct long narrow panels of constructed fabric which I alternated with bright red loosely woven cotton fabric.

This very bright vest (from the Cat-Crazy vest pattern by O'Dell House) coordinates well with denim pants, skirts, and dresses. The little patches are all different sizes and are uneven in width but they blend together in the long narrow panels. The width of your long strips will depend on the size of the fabric samples.

The vest is bound in black cotton and I painted some wavy lines across the red fabric bands with black slick fabric paint to tie the binding and body of the vest together.

The Guatemalan fabrics are heavy enough to eliminate the need for foundation fabric. However, they are very loosely woven, so handle them carefully to reduce the amount of raveling.

The Blues

Designed and sewn by Joyce Mori. The vest pattern is the In-Vest by Four Corners.

This vest features panels of blue crazy quilt constructed fabric. There are dark and dark/medium values but notice that many of the fabrics have white or very light motifs in them, which add variety and excitement to the vest.

The 4″ wide (finished size) panels of constructed fabric are separated by 1″ (finished size) strips of solid green fabric. The outside edges of the front sections are reinforced with interfacing.

The vest, made from the In-Vest pattern by Four Corners, is free-motion machine-quilted through all the layers with gold metallic thread which gives the garment extra body and eliminates the need for a foundation fabric.

Lavender Blues

Designed and sewn by Joyce Mori. The pattern is adapted from Lois Ericson's Vest Wardrobe #301.

The idea for Lavender Blues came from a T-shirt I purchased. The "vest" is really two vest fronts sewn on an oversized T-shirt. I used Lois Ericson's Vest Wardrobe #301 pattern for the vest fronts.

I used 2½″ panels (finished size) of blue constructed fabric, basically dark-value. Strips of a purple commercial fabric, 3″ wide (finished size), are sewn between the panels of constructed fabric and the completed pattern pieces are lined with a coordinating fabric just as you would line any vest. The front edge of each vest section is reinforced with interfacing to hold the shape.

I topstitched the vest pieces to the T-shirt shoulder edges by machine, but used hand-stitching to sew the vest on the T-shirt from the underarm seam down 4″towards the vest bottom. My T-shirt didn't have side seams, so I sewed the vest about 1½″ back from where the side seams would have been.

The remaining part of the side of the vest hangs free, which allows me to tuck the T-shirt into a skirt and have the vest hang over the front of the skirt's waistline, the way a real vest would.

Sophisticated Gray

Designed and sewn by Joyce Mori. The pattern is Crazy Quilt Vest by Debra Lunn.

Bright hand-dyed fabrics make up the small panels of constructed fabric which show up beautifully against the non-constructed gray background fabric with its mottled streaks and subtle shading.

The vest is sewn to a cotton foundation fabric cut ½″ larger around all the edges of the pattern pieces. Start at the top of each vest section and pin the first gray strip in place, then put the second gray strip down, right sides together, on the first strip and sew the seam, sewing through both strips and the foundation fabric. Flip the second strip down and iron it on the foundation fabric. Add a third gray strip and so on down the length of the vest.

When you have sewn all the strips to the foundation fabric, place the original pattern piece on the garment and trim the fabric to the correct size. Follow the pattern directions for putting the vest together. This vest is from Debra Lunn's Crazy Quilt Vest pattern. Debra's original version features patches of crazy quilt fabric along the front and bottom of the vest. Constructed fabric panels would work well in place of the crazy quilt fabric.

Fall Colors

Designed and sewn by Joyce Mori.

Constructed fabric can also be used on jackets and other garments. This jacket features constructed fabric for the sleeves, back yoke, pocket, and a strip on the left front. Notice that bias bar pieces (formed from the main fabric of the jacket) are appliqued across the pieces of constructed fabric to unify the main jacket fabric with the constructed fabric.

Pieces of constructed fabric for the yoke and front strip were sewn to a foundation fabric. The remaining fabric of the jacket was also sewn down on the foundation. Where the constructed fabric and regular fabric touched, the bias bar piece was sewn over this to cover the raw edges. As the bias bar was sewn down, the stitching caught all the layers, including the foundation fabric. For each sleeve, a piece of constructed fabric large enough to accom-

modate the sleeve pattern was sewn and the pattern was cut from this fabric. There is no foundation fabric in the sleeves.

Quilts

Gingham Dogs and Calico Cats

Designed, sewn, and machine-quilted by Pat Hill of West Hills, California.

This delightful baby quilt is a mix of soft pastel colors to fit in most nurseries, and it is an easy to sew project. (Constructed fabric type #9 in a medium-value crazy.)

Big X

This is the same design as Taste of Amish on page 60. Light constructed fabric forms the center of the quilt and the diagonal pieces

Designed, sewn, and machine-quilted by Joyce Mori.

feature medium- and dark-value constructed fabric, all framed with a dark blue border. This versatile quilt pattern can be colored in many different ways. Photocopy the drawing on page 96 to experiment with different color schemes. (Constructed fabric types #4, #2, and #10.)

Wild Jungle

Designed, sewn, and hand-quilted by Joyce Mori.

See the animal faces peering out from this exotic quilt? The solid colors used in the

constructed fabric blocks pick up the colors in the border, background, and block fabrics. Change the motif to an Autumn Leaves theme by substituting leaf print fabrics for the jungle ones. (Constructed fabric type #10 and #15.)

Crazy Country Tulip

Designed, sewn, and machine-quilted by Pat Hill of West Hills, California.

This cheery and colorful tulip is perfect for the kitchen or sun room to brighten even the gloomiest day. Notice how the leaves are shaded with medium and dark green constructed fabric. (Constructed fabric type #7.)

Crazy Contemporary Tulip

A collection of black and white printed fabric scraps contrast with the red solid fabric to make a sleek and contemporary tulip. Designer Pat Hill used silver metallic thread to zigzag around the edge of the tulip.

To really understand the possibilities of a

Designed, sewn, and machine-quilted by Pat Hill of West Hills, California.

design, it helps to work in a series—create several variations of the same design like Pat did with this series of tulip quilts. All the tulips are sewn with constructed fabric but the choice of colors makes each tulip unique. (Constructed fabric types #1 and #8.)

Crazy Southwestern Tulip

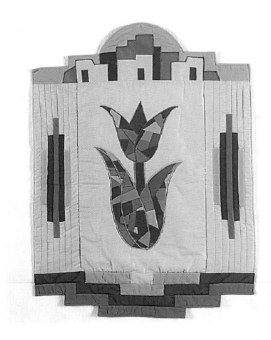

This quilt uses the colors of a Southwestern sunset. Notice the silhouette of a pueblo village at the top of the quilt and the Indian designs on the sides and bottom. (Constructed fabric type #16.)

A Taste of Amish, Triangles

Designed, sewn, and hand-quilted by Joyce Mori.

This quilt uses bright solid colors for the constructed fabric which are set off by the solid black fabric. Notice the narrow band of constructed fabric used as one of the borders. Compare this to A Taste of Amish on page 60, which has the same type of constructed fabric in a different design. (Constructed fabric type #16.)

Painted Stars

The stars in this quilt shade from dark to lighter in the corners. The constructed fabric is made from scraps of dyed and painted fabrics. The very nature of the dyed designs makes for interesting constructed fabric when viewed

Designed, sewn, and machine-quilted by Pat Hill of West Hills, California.

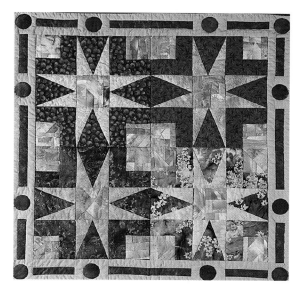

Designed and sewn by Joyce Mori and hand-quilted by Delores Stemple of Aurora, West Virginia.

close-up and from a distance.

The combination of colors and the designs on the dyed fabrics are truly one-of-a-kind and unusual, resulting in an extraordinary and striking new fabric. The unusual border on this quilt reinforces the almost futuristic look of the stars. (Constructed fabric type #7.)

Riot of Color

Designed and sewn by Joyce Mori and hand-quilted by Delores Stemple of Aurora, West Virginia.

No pastels here. The hand dyed fabrics used in the constructed fabric are boldly colored. Because I think of hand dyed fabrics as extra special, I don't like to waste even the smallest scrap and this design makes good use of these precious pieces of fabric. The sashing and border on this quilt are made from constructed fabric too. (Constructed fabric type #15.)

Blue Swirls

Designed and sewn by Joyce Mori.

Crazy quilt constructed fabric type #9 in light colors forms the center on point square made up of four triangles as part of the background for the easy to sew blue swirling motifs. Constructed fabric makes a wonderful background for appliqué work because it adds visual texture to the design. Just be careful not to create a background that has so much texture and pattern that the appliqué gets lost on top of it.

Appendix A
Line Drawings

The Star Block

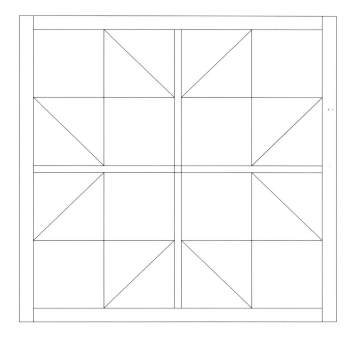

Purple Pinwheel

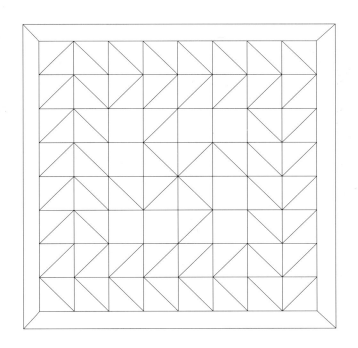

Slashing Squares

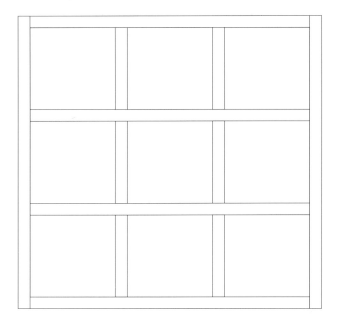

Turquoise Trail

An Art Quilt for Anyone

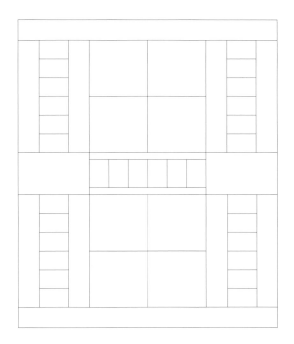

Diagonals

Squares: Solid and Hollow

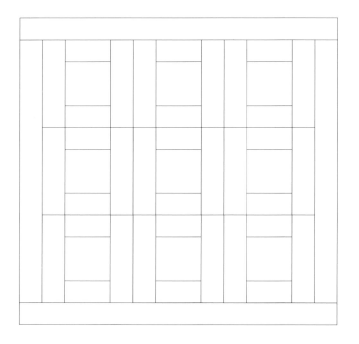

Gradations

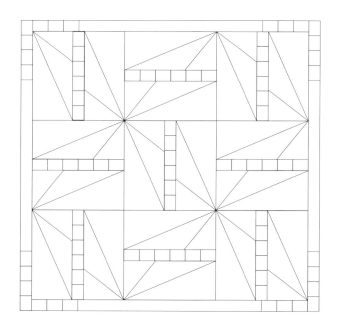

A Taste of Amish

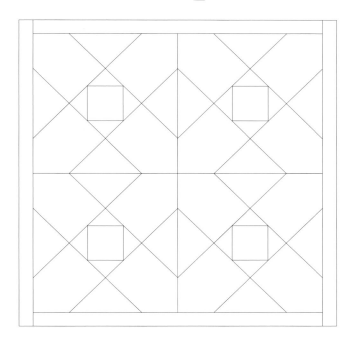

Serenity

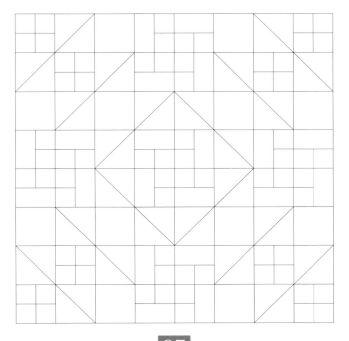

Peaceful Strips

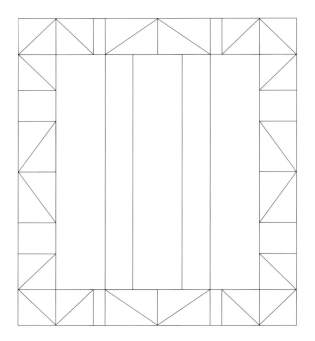

Country Charm

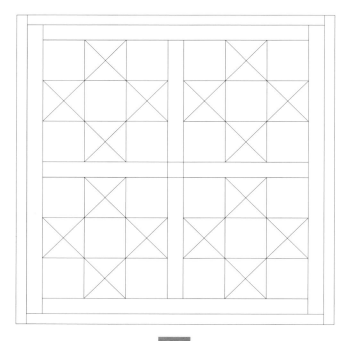

Bright Stars

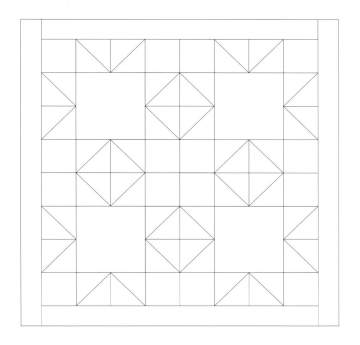

Colorful Sashing

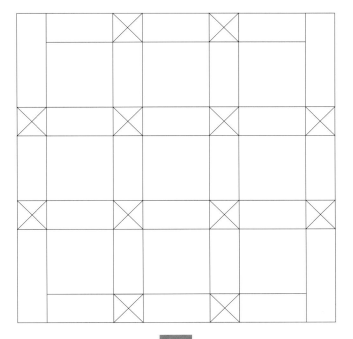

Southwestern Themes

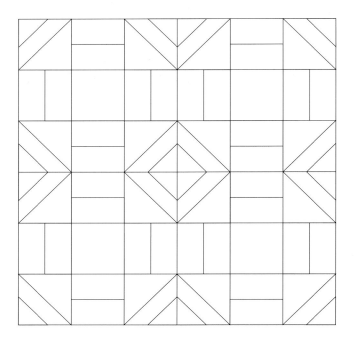

Shades of Red

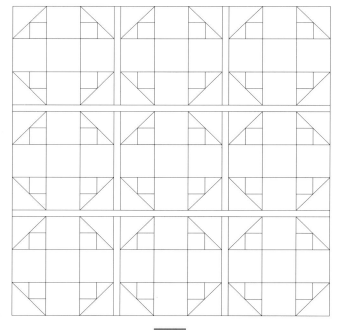

Appendix B
Templates

A

Star Block
Purple Pinwheel
Peaceful Strips

B

Shades of Red

C

Country Charm

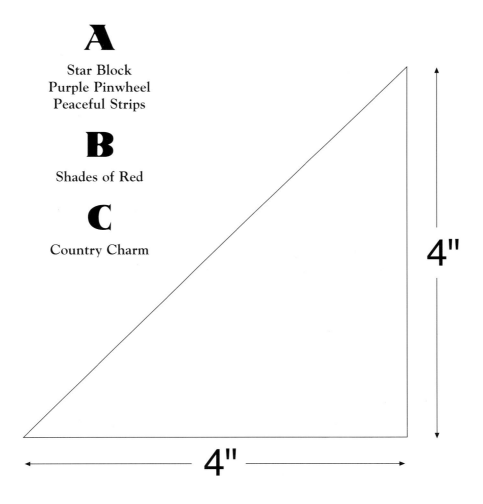

4"

4"

Add ¼" for seam allowances

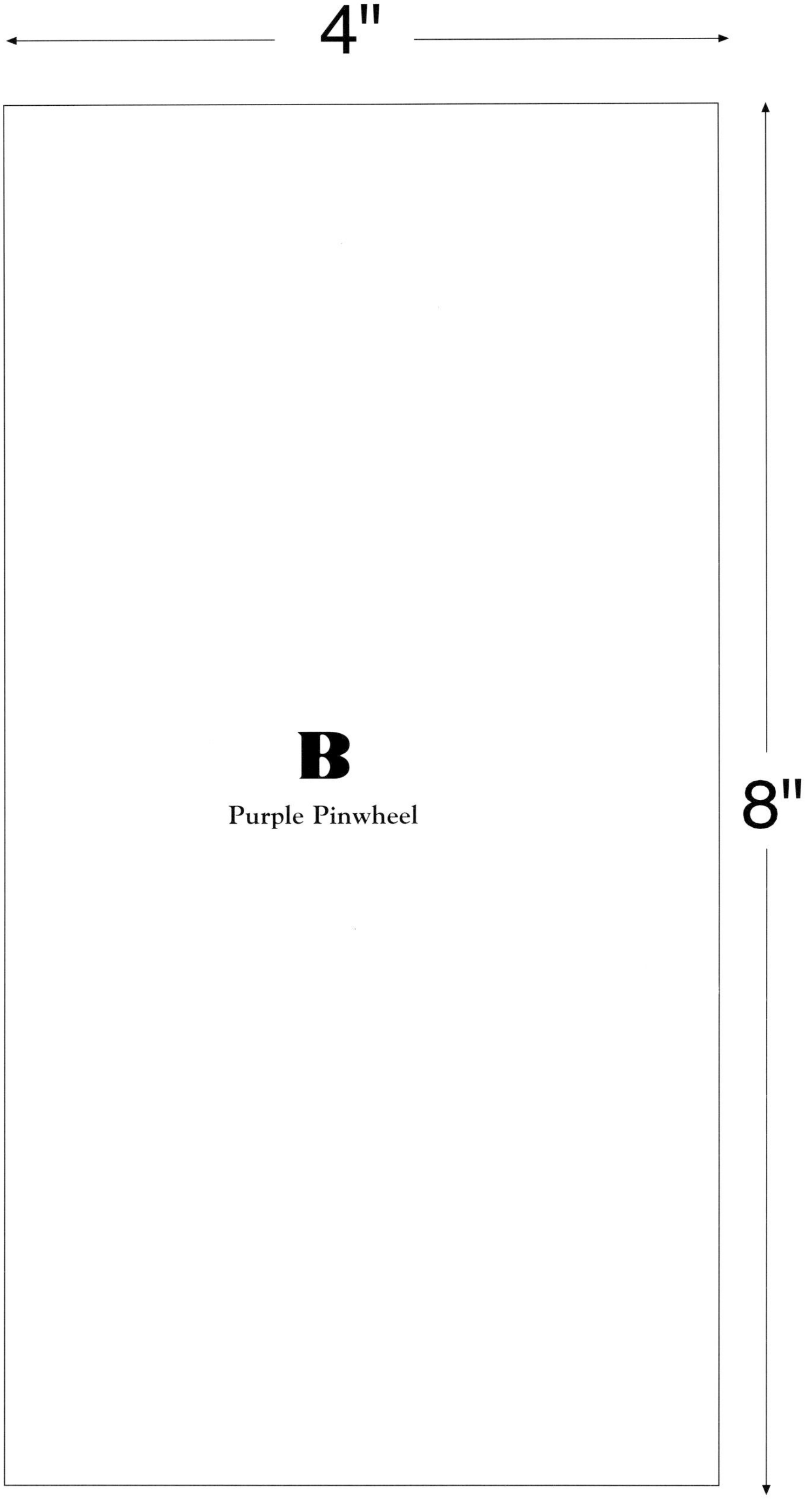

4"

B

Purple Pinwheel

8"

Add ¼" for seam allowances

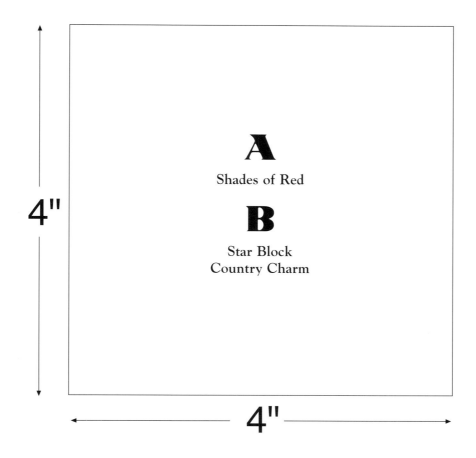

4"

4"

A

Shades of Red

B

Star Block
Country Charm

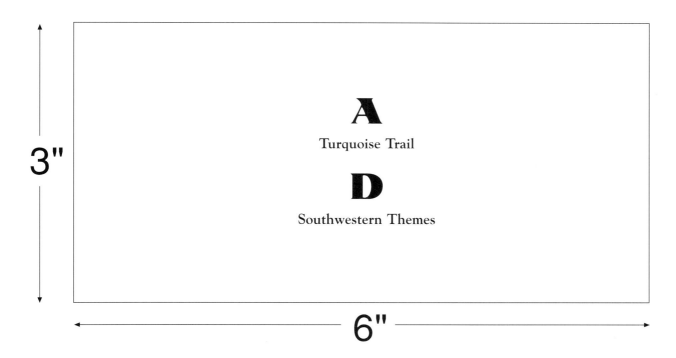

3"

6"

A

Turquoise Trail

D

Southwestern Themes

Add ¼" for seam allowances

6"

6"

A

Slashing Squares
An Art Quilt for Anyone
Diagonals
Bright Stars

E

Southwestern Themes

Add ¼" for seam allowances

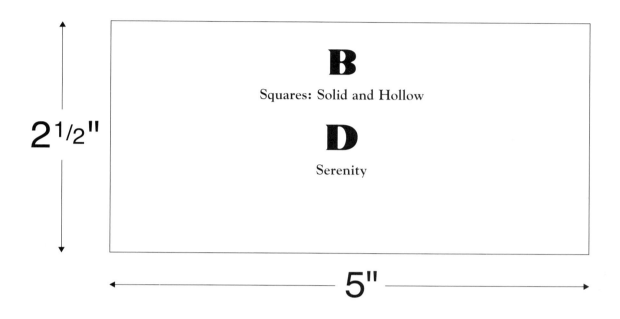

B

Squares: Solid and Hollow

D

Serenity

2½"

5"

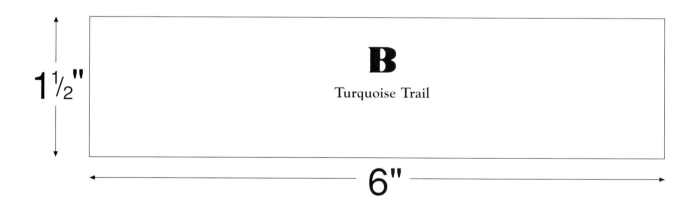

B

Turquoise Trail

1½"

6"

Add ¼" for seam allowances

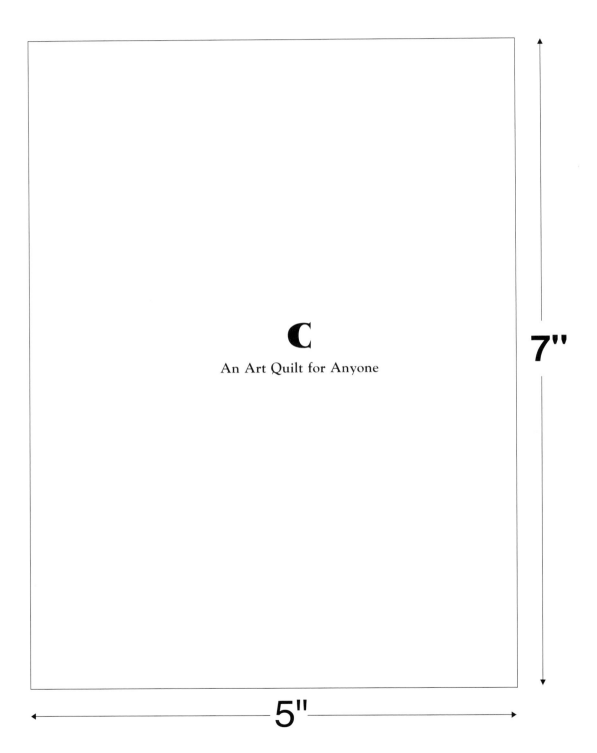

C

An Art Quilt for Anyone

7"

5"

Add ¼" for seam allowances

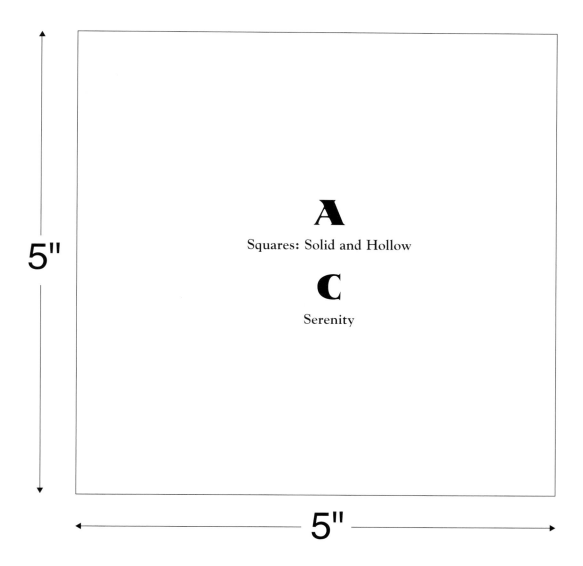

5"

5"

A

Squares: Solid and Hollow

C

Serenity

Add ¼" for seam allowances

C

Squares: Solid and Hollow

10"

2¹/₂"

Add ¼" for seam allowances

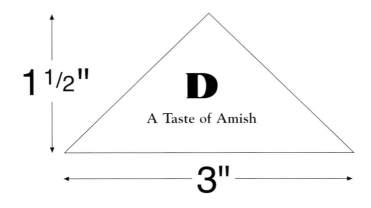

1 1/2"

D

A Taste of Amish

3"

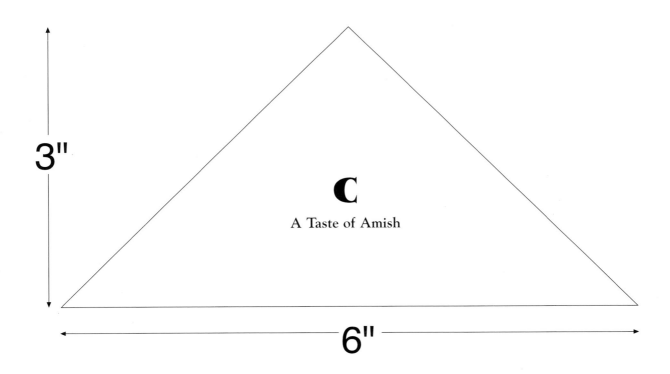

3"

C

A Taste of Amish

6"

Add ¼" for seam allowances

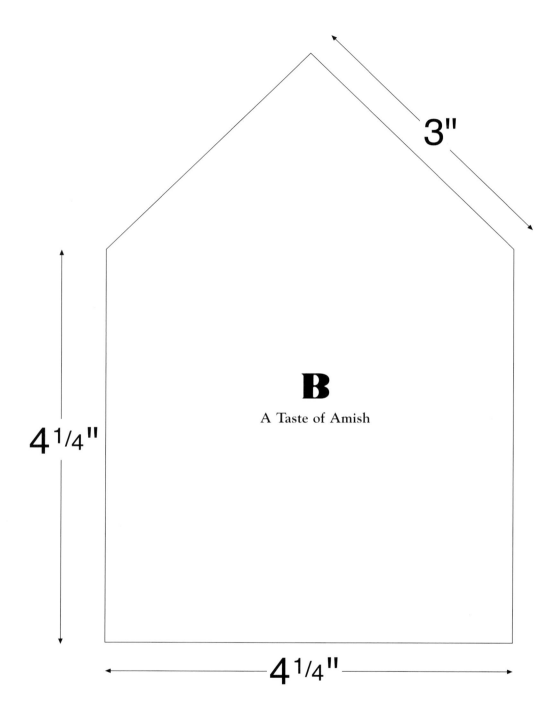

3"

B

A Taste of Amish

4 1/4"

4 1/4"

Add ¼" for seam allowances

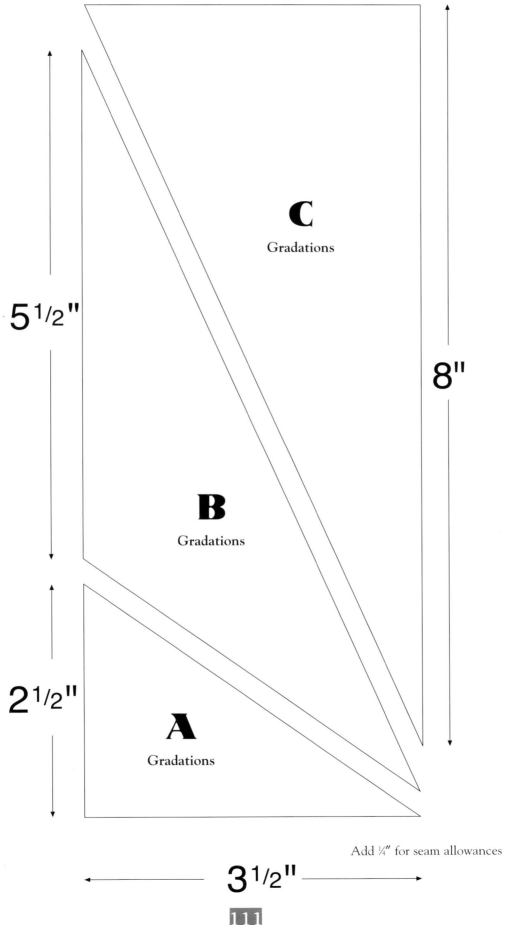

C
Gradations

5½"

8"

B
Gradations

2½"

A
Gradations

Add ¼" for seam allowances

3½"

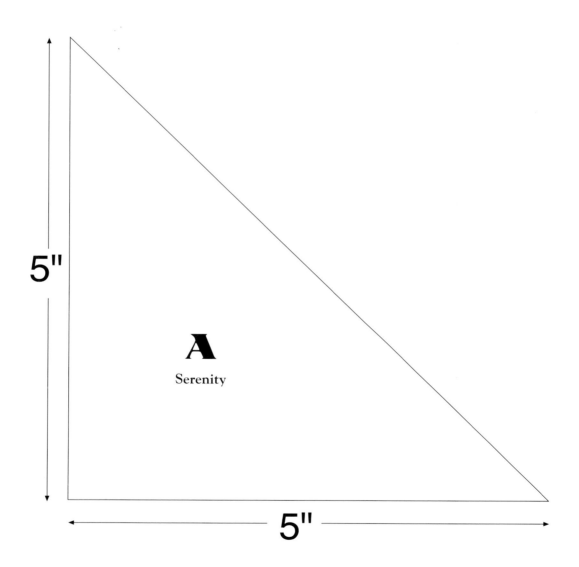

5"

5"

A

Serenity

Add ¼" for seam allowances

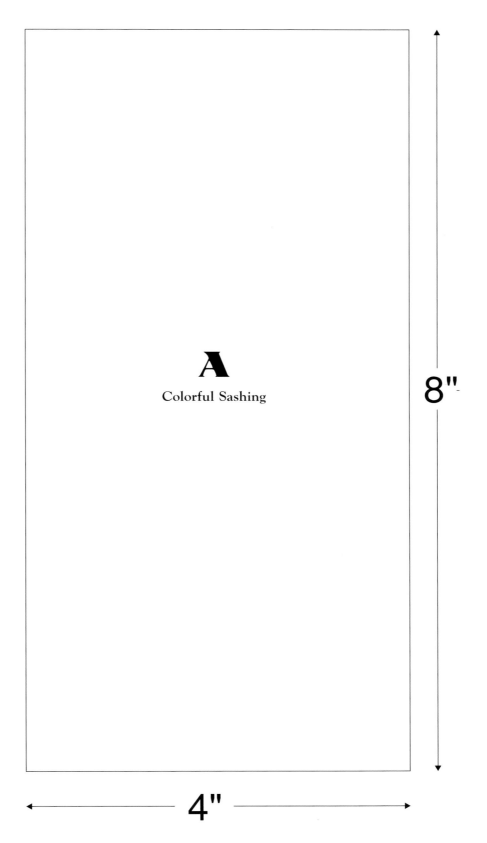

A

Colorful Sashing

8"

4"

Add ¼" for seam allowances

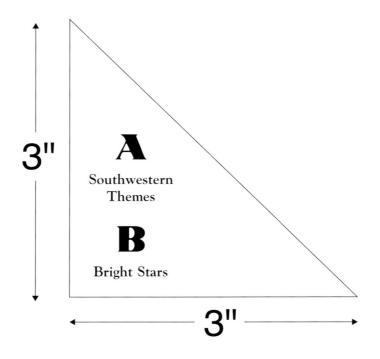

A

Southwestern
Themes

B

Bright Stars

3"

3"

B

An Art Quilt for Anyone

2"

3"

Add ¼" for seam allowances

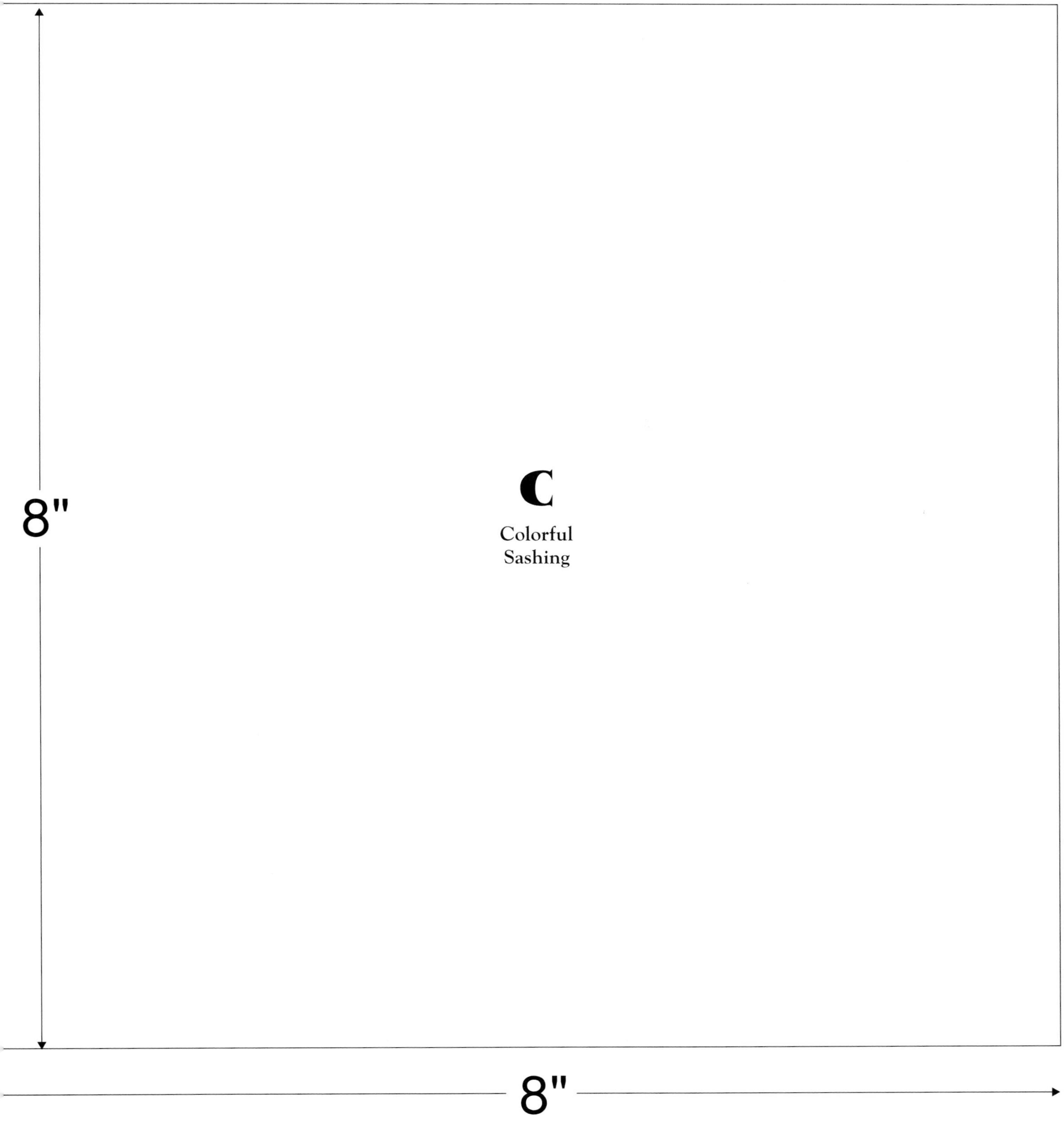

8"

8"

C

Colorful
Sashing

Add ¼" for seam allowances

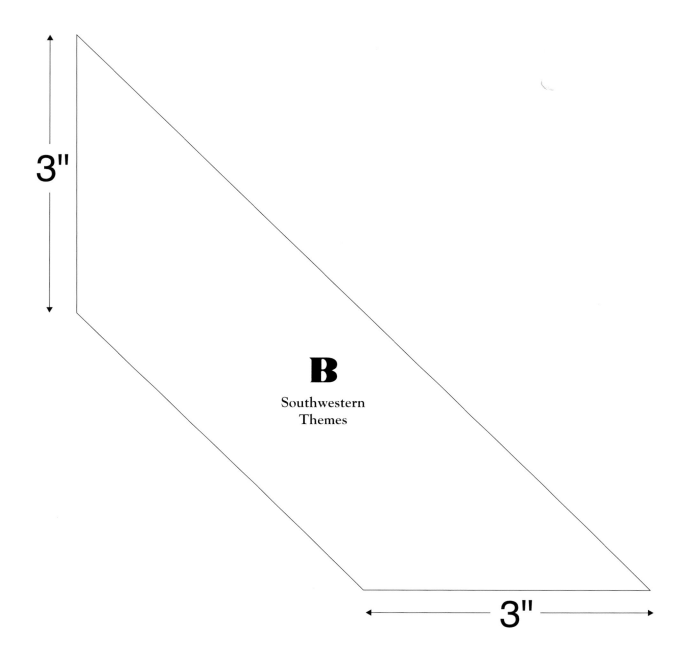

3"

B
Southwestern
Themes

3"

Add ¼" for seam allowances

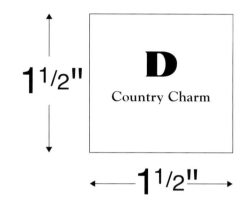

D

Country Charm

1^{1/2}"

1^{1/2}"

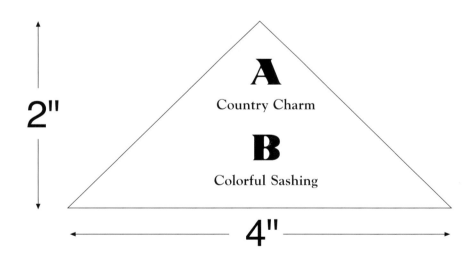

A

Country Charm

B

Colorful Sashing

2"

4"

Add ¼″ for seam allowances

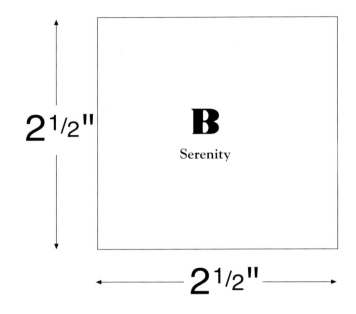

2 1/2"

2 1/2"

B

Serenity

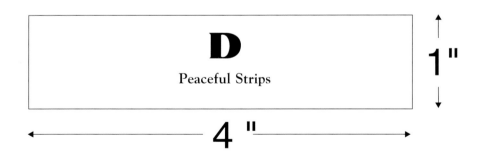

D

Peaceful Strips

1"

4 "

Add ¼" for seam allowances

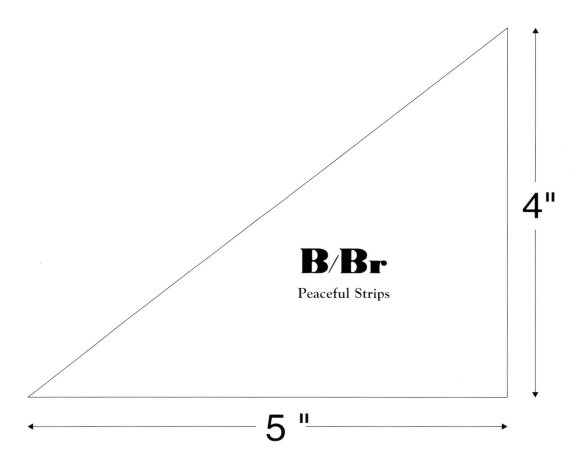

B/Br

Peaceful Strips

4"

5 "

Add ¼" for seam allowances

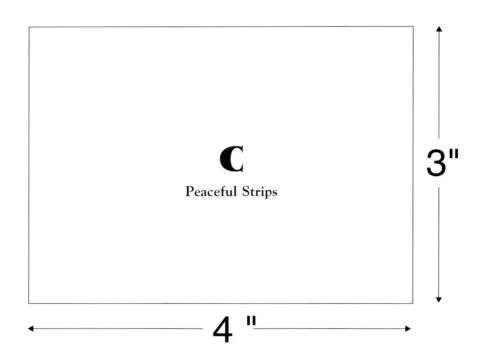

C

Peaceful Strips

3"

4 "

Add ¼" for seam allowances

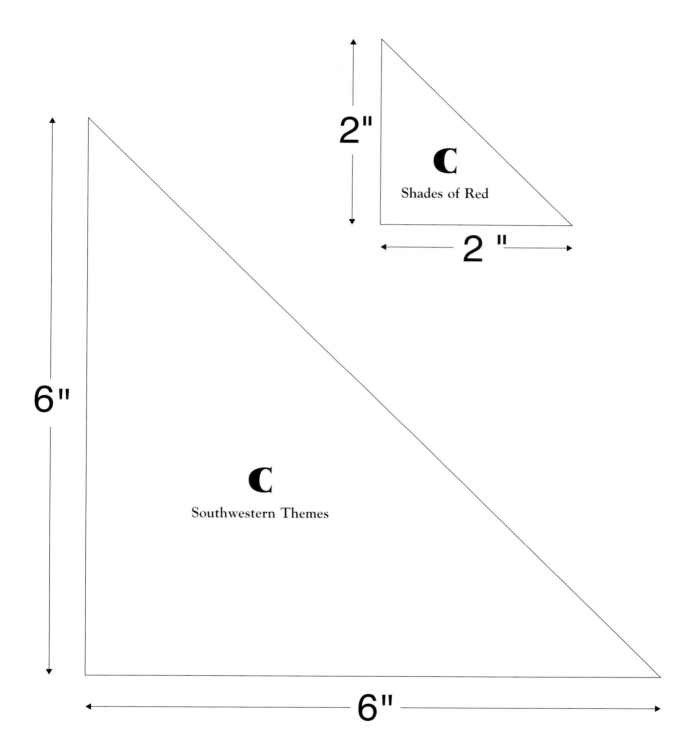

2"

C

Shades of Red

2 "

6"

C

Southwestern Themes

6"

Add ¼" for seam allowances

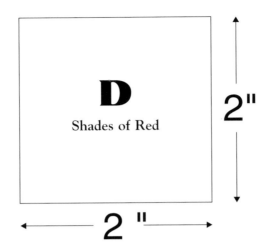

D

Shades of Red

2"

2 "

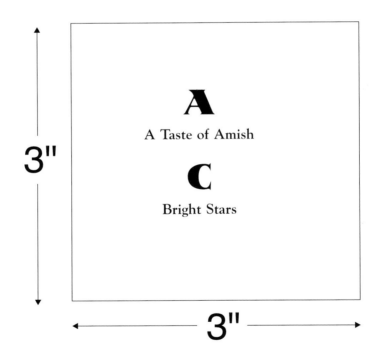

3"

A

A Taste of Amish

C

Bright Stars

3"

Add ¼" for seam allowances

Appendix C
Pattern Sources

Vest Wardrobe #301 by Lois Ericson
(used for Lavender Blues)

> Lois Ericson
> Box 5222
> Salem, OR   97304

Crazy Quilt Vest by Debra Lunn
(used for Sophisticated Gray)

> Debra Lunn
> 922 Madison Street
> Denver, CO   80206

Cat-Crazy Vest by O'Dell House
(used for Samples)

> O'Dell House
> 466 S. Odell
> Marshall, MO 65340

In-Vest by Four Corners
(used for The Blues)

> Four Corners
> 914 Loganwood
> Richardson, TX   75080

Index